Modern Critical Interpretations

Mary Shelley's Frankenstein

Modern Critical Interpretations

These and other titles in preparation

Modern Critical Interpretations

Mary Shelley's
Frankenstein

Edited and with an introduction by
Harold Bloom
Sterling Professor of the Humanities
Yale University

Chelsea House Publishers
NEW YORK ◊ PHILADELPHIA

Library of Congress Cataloging-in-Publication Data

Mary Shelley's Frankenstein.

(Modern critical interpretations)
Bibliography: p.
Includes index.
Summary: Seven critical essays bringing various
interpretations to the novel about a monster created
by a scientist.
1. Shelley, Mary Wollstonecraft, 1797–1851.
Frankenstein. [1. Shelley, Mary Wollstonecraft,
1797–1851. Frankenstein. 2. English literature—
History and criticism] I. Bloom, Harold. II. Series.
PR5397.F73M37   1987   823'.7   86-34296
ISBN 0–87754–746–7

Contents

Editor's Note

This book gathers together a representative selection of the best recent criticism of Mary Shelley's *Frankenstein*, arranged in the chronological order of its original publication. I am grateful to Shawn Rosenheim for his assistance as a researcher.

My introduction relates the novel both to Milton's *Paradise Lost* and to Percy Bysshe Shelley's Romantic Prometheanism. The chronological sequence of criticism begins with George Levine's complex essay that interprets Frankenstein's "monster" as a metaphor for the strategies of realism, and so as setting a pattern for novelists as recent and strong as Joseph Conrad.

In an investigation of creation as catastrophe, Paul Sherwin integrates *Frankenstein* with its full context in High Romantic literature. Barbara Johnson deconstructs *Frankenstein* so as to reveal that "the monstrousness of selfhood is intimately embedded within the question of female autobiography." For the novelist Joyce Carol Oates, Mary Shelley's narrative is "the picture of a finite and flawed god at war with, and eventually overcome by, his creation."

In the reading of the feminist critic Mary Poovey, Mary Shelley underwent a transition from aggressive and ambitious imagination to the desire to disguise that aggression in the persona of a "proper lady." The image of the father in *Frankenstein* receives a psychoanalytical exegesis from William Veeder, after which Margaret Homans ends this volume with an essay on the absence of the maternal image in Mary Shelley's still disturbing fantasy.

Introduction

there is a fire
And motion of the soul which will not dwell
In its own narrow being, but aspire
Beyond the fitting medium of desire.
BYRON. *Childe Harold's Pilgrimage,* canto 3

Ere Babylon was dust,
The Magus Zoroaster, my dead child,
Met his own image walking in the garden.
That apparition, sole of men, he saw.
For know there are two worlds of life and death:
One that which thou beholdest; but the other
Is underneath the grave, where do inhabit
The shadows of all forms that think and live
Till death unite them and they part no more
SHELLEY. *Prometheus Unbound,* act 1

The motion-picture viewer who carries his obscure but still authentic taste for the sublime to the neighborhood theater, there to see the latest in an unending series of *Frankensteins*, becomes a sharer in a romantic terror now nearly one hundred and fifty years old. Mary Shelley, barely nineteen years of age when she wrote the original *Frankenstein*, was the daughter of two great intellectual rebels, William Godwin and Mary Wollstonecraft, and the second wife of Percy Bysshe Shelley, another great rebel and an unmatched lyrical poet. Had she written nothing, Mary Shelley would be remembered today. She is remembered in her own right as the author of a novel valuable in itself but also prophetic of an intellectual world to come, a novel depicting a Prometheanism that is with us still.

"Frankenstein," to most of us, is the name of a monster rather than of a monster's creator, for the common reader and the common

1

viewer have worked together, in their apparent confusion, to create a myth soundly based on a central duality in Mary Shelley's novel. A critical discussion of *Frankenstein* needs to begin from an insight first recorded by Richard Church and Muriel Spark: the monster and his creator are the antithetical halves of a single being. Spark states the antithesis too cleanly; for her Victor Frankenstein represents the feelings, and his nameless creature the intellect. In her view the monster has no emotion, and "what passes for emotion . . . are really intellectual passions arrived at through rational channels." Spark carries this argument far enough to insist that the monster is asexual and that he demands a bride from Frankenstein only for companionship, a conclusion evidently at variance with the novel's text.

The antithesis between the scientist and his creature in *Frankenstein* is a very complex one and can be described more fully in the larger context of Romantic literature and its characteristic mythology. The shadow or double of the self is a constant conceptual image in Blake and Shelley and a frequent image, more random and descriptive, in the other major Romantics, especially in Byron. In *Frankenstein* it is the dominant and recurrent image and accounts for much of the latent power the novel possesses.

Mary Shelley's husband was a divided being, as man and as poet, just as his friend Byron was, though in Shelley the split was more radical. *Frankenstein; or, The Modern Prometheus* is the full title of Mary Shelley's novel, and while Victor Frankenstein is *not* Shelley (Clerval is rather more like the poet), the Modern Prometheus is a very apt term for Shelley or for Byron. Prometheus is the mythic figure who best suits the uses of Romantic poetry, for no other traditional being has in him the full range of Romantic moral sensibility and the full Romantic capacity for creation and destruction.

No Romantic writer employed the Prometheus archetype without a full awareness of its equivocal potentialities. The Prometheus of the ancients had been for the most part a spiritually reprehensible figure, though frequently a sympathetic one, in terms both of his dramatic situation and in his close alliance with mankind against the gods. But this alliance had been ruinous for man in most versions of the myth, and the Titan's benevolence toward humanity was hardly sufficient recompense for the alienation of man from heaven that he had brought about. Both sides of Titanism are evident in earlier Christian references to the story. The same Prometheus who is taken as an analogue of the crucified Christ is regarded also as a type of Lucifer, a son of light justly cast out by an offended heaven.

In the Romantic readings of Milton's *Paradise Lost* (and *Frankenstein* is implicitly one such reading) this double identity of Prometheus is a vital element. Blake, whose mythic revolutionary named Orc is another version of Prometheus, saw Milton's Satan as a Prometheus gone wrong, as desire restrained until it became only the shadow of desire, a diminished double of creative energy. Shelley went further in judging Milton's Satan as an imperfect Prometheus, inadequate because his mixture of heroic and base qualities engendered in the reader's mind a "pernicious casuistry" inimical to the spirit of art.

Blake, more systematic a poet than Shelley, worked out an antithesis between symbolic figures he named Spectre and Emanation, the shadow of desire and the total form of desire, respectively. A reader of *Frankenstein*, recalling the novel's extraordinary conclusion, with its scenes of obsessional pursuit through the Arctic wastes, can recognize the same imagery applied to a similar symbolic situation in Blake's lyric on the strife of Spectre and Emanation:

> My Spectre around me night and day
> Like a Wild beast guards my way.
> My Emanation far within
> Weeps incessantly for my Sin.
>
> A Fathomless and boundless deep,
> There we wander, there we weep;
> On the hungry craving wind
> My Spectre follows thee behind.
>
> He scents thy footsteps in the snow,
> Wheresoever thou dost go
> Thro' the wintry hail and rain.

Frankenstein's monster, tempting his revengeful creator on through a world of ice, is another Emanation pursued by a Spectre, with the enormous difference that he is an Emanation flawed, a nightmare of actuality, rather than dream of desire. Though abhorred rather than loved, the monster is the total form of Frankenstein's creative power and is *more imaginative* than his creator. The monster is at once more intellectual and more emotional than his maker; indeed he excels Frankenstein as much (and in the same ways) as Milton's Adam excels

Milton's God in *Paradise Lost*. The greatest paradox and most astonishing achievement of Mary Shelley's novel is that the monster is *more human* than his creator. This nameless being, as much a Modern Adam as his creator is a Modern Prometheus, is more lovable than his creator and more hateful, more to be pitied and more to be feared, and above all more able to give the attentive reader that shock of added consciousness in which aesthetic recognition compels a heightened realization of the self. For like Blake's Spectre and Emanation or Shelley's Alastor and Epipsyche, Frankenstein and his monster are the solipsistic and generous halves of the one self. Frankenstein is the mind and emotions turned in upon themselves, and his creature is the mind and emotions turned imaginatively outward, seeking a greater humanization through a confrontation of other selves.

I am suggesting that what makes *Frankenstein* an important book, though it is only a strong, flawed novel with frequent clumsiness in its narrative and characterization, is that it contains one of the most vivid versions we have of the Romantic mythology of the self, one that resembles Blakes's *Book of Urizen*, Shelley's *Prometheus Unbound*, and Byron's *Manfred*, among other works. Because it lacks the sophistication and imaginative complexity of such works, *Frankenstein* affords a unique introduction to the archetypal world of the Romantics.

William Godwin, though a tendentious novelist, was a powerful one, and the prehistory of his daughter's novel begins with his best work of fiction, *Caleb Williams* (1794). Godwin summarized the climactic (and harrowing) final third of his novel as a pattern of flight and pursuit, "the fugitive in perpetual apprehension of being overwhelmed with the worst calamities, and the pursuer, by his ingenuity and resources, keeping his victim in a state of the most fearful alarm." Mary Shelley brilliantly reverses this pattern in the final sequence of her novel, and she takes from *Caleb Williams* also her destructive theme of the monster's war against "the whole machinery of human society," to quote the words of Caleb Williams while in prison. Muriel Spark argues that *Frankenstein* can be read as a reaction "against the rational-humanism of Godwin and Shelley," and she points to the equivocal preface that Shelley wrote to his wife's novel, in order to support this view. Certainly Shelley was worried lest the novel be taken as a warning against the inevitable moral consequences of an unchecked experimental Prometheanism and scientific materialism. The preface insists that:

The opinions which naturally spring from the character and situation of the hero are by no means to be conceived as existing always in my own conviction; nor is any inference justly to be drawn from the following pages as prejudicing any philosophical doctrine of whatever kind.

Shelley had, throughout his own work, a constant reaction against Godwin's rational humanism, but his reaction was systematically and consciously one of heart against head. In the same summer in the Swiss Alps that saw the conception of *Frankenstein*, Shelley composed two poems that lift the thematic conflict of the novel to the level of the true sublime. In the "Hymn to Intellectual Beauty" the poet's heart interprets an inconstant grace and loveliness, always just beyond the range of the human senses, as being the only beneficent force in life, and he prays to this force to be more constant in its attendance upon him and all mankind. In a greater sister-hymn, "Mont Blanc," an awesome meditation upon a frightening natural scene, the poet's head issues an allied but essentially contrary report. The force, or power, is there, behind or within the mountain, but its external workings upon us are either indifferent or malevolent, and this power is not to be prayed to. It can teach us, but what it teaches us is our own dangerous freedom from nature, the necessity for our will to become a significant part of materialistic necessity. Though "Mont Blanc" works its way to an almost heroic conclusion, it is also a poem of horror and reminds us that Frankenstein first confronts his conscious monster in the brooding presence of Mont Blanc, and to the restless music of one of Shelley's lyrics of Mutability.

In *Prometheus Unbound* the split between head and heart is not healed, but the heart is allowed dominance. The hero, Prometheus, like Frankenstein, has made a monster, but this monster is Jupiter, the God of all institutional and historical religions, including organized Christianity. Salvation from this conceptual error comes through love alone; but love in this poem, as elsewhere in Shelley, is always closely shadowed by ruin. Indeed, what choice spirits in Shelley perpetually encounter is ruin masquerading as love, pain presenting itself as pleasure. The tentative way out of this situation in Shelley's poetry is through the quest for a feeling mind and an understanding heart, which is symbolized by the sexual reunion of Prometheus and his Emanation, Asia. Frederick A. Pottle sums up *Prometheus Unbound* by observing its meaning to be that "the head must sincerely forgive, must willingly eschew hatred on purely experimental grounds," while "the affections must exorcize the demons of infancy, whether personal or of the race." In the light cast by these profound and precise summations, the reader can better understand both Shelley's lyrical drama and his wife's narrative of the Modern Prometheus.

There are two paradoxes at the center of Mary Shelley's novel, and each illuminates a dilemma of the Promethean imagination. The first is that Frankenstein *was* successful, in that he did create Natural Man, not as he was, but as the meliorists saw such a man; indeed, Frankenstein did better than this, since his creature was, as we have seen, more imaginative than himself. Frankenstein's tragedy stems not from his Promethean excess but from his own moral error, his failure to love; he *abhorred his creature*, became terrified, and fled his responsibilities.

The second paradox is the more ironic. This either would not have happened or would not have mattered anyway, if Frankenstein had been an aesthetically successful maker; a beautiful "monster," or even a passable one, would not have been a monster. As the creature bitterly observes in chapter 17,

> Shall I respect man when he contemns me? Let him live with me in the interchange of kindness, and instead of injury I would bestow every benefit upon him with tears of gratitude at his acceptance. But that cannot be; the human senses are insurmountable barriers to our union.

As the hideousness of his creature was no part of Victor Frankenstein's intention, it is worth noticing how this disastrous matter came to be.

It would not be unjust to characterize Victor Frankenstein, in his act of creation, as being momentarily a moral idiot, like so many who have done his work after him. There is an indeliberate humor in the contrast between the enormity of the scientist's discovery and the mundane emotions of the discoverer. Finding that "the minuteness of the parts" slows him down, he resolves to make his creature "about eight feet in height and proportionably large." As he works on, he allows himself to dream that "a new species would bless me as its creator and source; many happy and excellent natures would owe their being to me." Yet he knows his is a "workshop of filthy creation," and he fails the fundamental test of his own creativity. When the "dull yellow eye" of his creature opens, this creator falls from the autonomy of a supreme artificer to the terror of a child of earth: "breathless horror and disgust filled my heart." He flees his responsibility and sets in motion the events that will lead to his own Arctic immolation, a fit end for a being who has never achieved a full sense of another's existence.

Haunting Mary Shelley's novel is the demonic figure of the Ancient Mariner, Coleridge's major venture into Romantic mythology of the purgatorial self trapped in the isolation of a heightened self-consciousness. Walton, in Letter 2 introducing the novel, compares himself "to that production of the most imaginative of modern poets." As a seeker-out of an unknown passage, Walton is himself a Promethean quester, like Frankenstein, toward whom he is so compellingly drawn. Coleridge's Mariner is of the line of Cain, and the irony of Frankenstein's fate is that he too is a Cain, involuntarily murdering all his loved ones through the agency of his creature. The Ancient Mariner is punished by living under the curse of his consciousness of guilt, while the excruciating torment of Frankenstein is never to be able to forget his guilt in creating a lonely consciousness driven to crime by the rage of unwilling solitude.

It is part of Mary Shelley's insight into her mythological theme that all the monster's victims are innocents. The monster not only refuses actively to slay his guilty creator, he *mourns* for him, though with the equivocal tribute of terming the scientist a "generous and self-devoted being." Frankenstein, the modern Prometheus who has violated nature, receives his epitaph from the ruined second nature he has made, the God-abandoned, who consciously echoes the ruined Satan of *Paradise Lost* and proclaims, "Evil thenceforth became my good." It is imaginatively fitting that the greater and more interesting consciousness of the creature should survive his creator, for he alone in Mary Shelley's novel possesses character. Frankenstein, like Coleridge's Mariner, has no character in his own right; both figures win a claim to our attention only by their primordial crimes against original nature.

The monster is of course Mary Shelley's finest invention, and his narrative (chaps. 11–16) forms the highest achievement of the novel, more absorbing even than the magnificent and almost surrealistic pursuit of the climax. In an age so given to remarkable depictions of the dignity of natural man, an age including the shepherds and beggars of Wordsworth and what W. J. Bate has termed Keats's "polar ideal of disinterestedness"—even in such a literary time Frankenstein's hapless creature stands out as a sublime embodiment of heroic pathos. Though

Frankenstein lacks the moral imagination to understand him, the daemon's appeal is to what is most compassionate in us:

> Oh, Frankenstein, be not equitable to every other, and tram-
> ple upon me alone, to whom thy justice, and even thy
> clemency and affection, is most due. Remember that I am
> thy creature; *I ought to be thy Adam, but I am rather the fallen*
> *angel, whom thou drivest from joy for no misdeed.* Everywhere I
> see bliss, from which I alone am irrevocably excluded. I was
> benevolent and good; misery made me a fiend. Make me
> happy, and I shall again be virtuous.

The passage I have italicized is the imaginative kernel of the novel
and is meant to remind the reader of the novel's epigraph:

> Did I request thee, Maker, from my clay
> To mold me man? Did I solicit thee
> From darkness to promote me?

That desperate plangency of the fallen Adam becomes the characteristic accent of the daemon's lamentations, with the influence of
Milton cunningly built into the novel's narrative by the happy device
of Frankenstein's creature receiving his education through reading *Paradise Lost* as "a true history." Already doomed because his standards
are human, which makes him an outcast even to himself, his Miltonic
education completes his fatal growth in self-consciousness. His story,
as told to his maker, follows a familiar Romantic pattern "of the
progress of my intellect," as he puts it. His first pleasure after the
dawn of consciousness comes through his wonder at seeing the moon
rise. Caliban-like, he responds wonderfully to music, both natural and
human, and his sensitivity to the natural world has the responsiveness
of an incipient poet. His awakening to a first love for other beings, the
inmates of the cottage he haunts, awakens him also to the great
desolation of love rejected when he attempts to reveal himself. His
own duality of situation and character, caught between the states of
Adam and Satan, Natural Man and his thwarted desire, is related by
him directly to his reading of Milton's epic:

> It moved every feeling of wonder and awe that the picture
> of an omnipotent God warring with his creatures was capa-
> ble of exciting. I often referred the several situations, as their
> similarity struck me, to my own. Like Adam, I was appar-

ently united by no link to any other being in existence, but his state was far different from mine in every other respect. He had come forth from the hands of God a perfect creature, happy and prosperous, guarded by the especial care of his Creator; he was allowed to converse with and acquire knowledge from beings of a superior nature; but I was wretched, helpless, and alone. Many times I considered Satan as the fitter emblem of my condition, for often, like him, when I viewed the bliss of my protectors, the bitter gall of envy rose within me.

From a despair this profound, no release is possible. Driven forth into an existence upon which "the cold stars shone in mockery," the daemon declares "everlasting war against the species" and enters upon a fallen existence more terrible than the expelled Adam's. Echoing Milton, he asks the ironic question "And now, with the world before me, whither should I bend my steps?" to which the only possible answer is, toward his wretched Promethean creator.

If we stand back from Mary Shelley's novel in order better to view its archetypal shape, we see it as the quest of a solitary and ravaged consciousness first for consolation, then for revenge, and finally for a self-destruction that will be apocalyptic, that will bring down the creator with his creature. Though Mary Shelley may not have intended it, her novel's prime theme is a necessary counterpoise to Prometheanism, for Prometheanism exalts the increase in consciousness despite all cost. Frankenstein breaks through the barrier that separates man from God and gives apparent life, but in doing so he gives only death-in-life. The profound dejection endemic in Mary Shelley's novel is fundamental to the Romantic mythology of the self, for all Romantic horrors are diseases of excessive consciousness, of the self unable to bear the self. Kierkegaard remarks that Satan's despair is absolute because Satan, as pure spirit, is pure consciousness, and for Satan (and all men in his predicament) every increase in consciousness is an increase in despair. Frankenstein's desperate creature attains the state of pure spirit through his extraordinary situation and is racked by a consciousness in which every thought is a fresh disease.

A Romantic poet fought against self-consciousness through the strength of what he called imagination, a more than rational energy by which thought could seek to heal itself. But Frankenstein's daemon, though he is in the archetypal situation of the Romantic Wanderer or

Solitary, who sometimes was a poet, can win no release from his own story by telling it. His desperate desire for a mate is clearly an attempt to find a Shelleyan Epipsyche or Blakean Emanation for himself, a self within the self. But as he is the nightmare actualization of Frankenstein's desire, he is himself an emanation of Promethean yearnings, and his only double is his creator and denier.

When Coleridge's Ancient Mariner progressed from the purgatory of consciousness to his very minimal control of imagination, he failed to save himself, since he remained in a cycle of remorse, but he at least became a salutary warning to others and made of the Wedding Guest a wiser and a better man. Frankenstein's creature can help neither himself nor others, for he has no natural ground to which he can return. Romantic poets liked to return to the imagery of the ocean of life and immortality, for in the eddying to and fro of the healing waters they could picture a hoped-for process of restoration, of a survival of consciousness despite all its agonies. Mary Shelley, with marvelous appropriateness, brings her Romantic novel to a demonic conclusion in a world of ice. The frozen sea is the inevitable emblem for both the wretched daemon and his obsessed creator, but the daemon is allowed a final image of reversed Prometheanism. There is a heroism fully earned in the being who cries farewell in a claim of sad triumph: "I shall ascend my funeral pile triumphantly and exult in the agony of the torturing flames." Mary Shelley could not have known how dark a prophecy this consummation of consciousness would prove to be for the two great Promethean poets who were at her side during the summer of 1816, when her novel was conceived. Byron, writing his own epitaph at Missolonghi in 1824, and perhaps thinking back to having stood at Shelley's funeral pile two years before, found an image similar to the daemon's to sum up an exhausted existence:

> The fire that on my bosom preys
> Is lone as some volcanic isle;
> No torch is kindled at its blaze—
> A funeral pile.

The fire of increased consciousness stolen from heaven ends as an isolated volcano cut off from other selves by an estranging sea. "The light of that conflagration will fade away; my ashes will be swept into the sea by the winds" is the exultant cry of Frankenstein's creature. A blaze at which no torch is kindled is Byron's self-image, but he ends his death poem on another note, the hope for a soldier's grave, which he found. There is no Promethean release, but release is perhaps not the burden of the literature of Romantic aspiration. There is something both Godwinian and Shelleyan about the final utterance of Victor Frankenstein, which is properly made to Walton, the failed Promethean whose ship has just turned back. Though chastened, the Modern Prometheus ends with a last word true, not to his accomplishment, but to his desire:

> Farewell, Walton! Seek happiness in tranquillity and avoid ambition, even if it be only the apparently innocent one of distinguishing yourself in science and discoveries. Yet why do I say this? I have myself been blasted in these hopes, yet another may succeed.

Shelley's Prometheus, crucified on his icy precipice, found his ultimate torment in a Fury's taunt: "And all best things are thus confused to ill." It seems a fitting summation for all the work done by modern Prometheanism and might have served as an alternate epigraph for Mary Shelley's disturbing novel.

The Pattern: *Frankenstein* and Austen to Conrad

George Levine

> By God, I hope I shal you telle a thing
> That shal by reson been at your liking;
> For though myself be a ful vicious man,
> A moral tale yit I you can telle.
> CHAUCER'S PARDONER

Beginnings and endings . . . are arbitrary, and chronology falsely presumes meaningful traditions and influences. This study borrows from the shape of chronology, primarily because I am more concerned with the way writers in the realist tradition imagined their relation to each other, to the form of the novel, and to their culture's imagination of knowledge, than I am with the antichronological implications of the fulfilled realist intention. Realism leads away from its originating structures, not to closure, but to indeterminacy, not to clarified relation between idea and thing, but to their exclusiveness. To provide a framework for the studies that follow, I offer here something of a narrative, a tale starting with Mary Shelley's *Frankenstein*, which provides both a pattern and a metaphor for the very different realist literature that followed, and taking as its chronological extremes Jane Austen and Joseph Conrad, figures representative of the polarities of the realist impulse. With the figure of some monster emergent from the most stable as from the most volatile realist texts, we find every writer before Conrad touching on the skeptical possibilities he dramatized, every one after Austen seeking the controlling form she imag-

From *The Realistic Imagination: English Fiction from* Frankenstein *to* Lady Chatterley.
© 1981 by the University of Chicago. University of Chicago Press, 1981.

ined in the communal recognition of the ordinary. The critical narrative I imagine here is therefore presented as a fiction whose closure emphasizes the distance between it and the truth it seeks, metonymically, to shadow forth.

> *This nameless mode of naming the unnameable is rather good.*
> MARY SHELLEY

Frankenstein and his monster will turn up frequently . . . because in their curious relationship they enact much that is central to the traditions of realistic narrative, but much that is not quite reducible to discursive prose. Sandra Gilbert and Susan Gubar identify as a characteristic of women's literature the projection of "what seems to be the energy of their own despair into passionate, even melodramatic characters who act out the subversive impulses every woman feels when she contemplates the 'deep-rooted evils of patriarchy.' " *Frankenstein*, of course, provides a perfect model for this; but as I have tried to suggest elsewhere in an extensive analysis of the novel, it provides a model for the whole tradition of realism that I have been identifying. It is true that "even the most apparently conservative and decorous women writers" create such figures. But it is no accident that conservative male writers within the tradition of nineteenth-century realism do so as well. For realism embodies in its very texture the controlling force of the established order of society and history; it is thus a mode particularly available to women writers, sensitive to such force, as Gilbert and Gubar show them to be. It is also, however a mode appropriate to any writers who share women's ambivalence about established authority—needing the very structures that are felt to be oppressive and narrow. Such ambivalence is characteristic of almost every important Victorian writer.

Nineteenth-century realistic fiction tends to be concerned with the possibility of accommodation to established power, and yet, given its inevitable interest in character, it explores with at least equal intensity the possibility of resistance as well. The "madwoman in the attic," to use Gilbert and Gubar's phrase, has her male counterpart; the domesticated man—Pip, Pendennis, or Edward Waverley—has his dangerously rebellious double. Female resistance to the patriarch is echoed in a general Victorian resistance to the tyranny of society, of convention, of the majority.

Mary Shelley's characters, the monster and his creator, reflect the culture's ambivalence about itself, the realist's difficulty with the narrative conventions of realism. As creator, Frankenstein attempts to reach beyond the limits of human possibility, as the realists reached beyond words, into reality. Yet when he finds what his imagination has brought forth, he recoils from it as monstrous, and denies kinship. Thus denied, the monster in effect destroys all that belongs to a recognizably domestic world: the child, the caring friend, the affectionate servant, the all-providing father (whose death he only indirectly causes) and, most important, the bride on her wedding night. The consummation of community, the confirmation of a justly ordered world, the affirmation of consonance between word and action, the marriage turns out to be a murder. All the potential horrors of domestic realism, so carefully averted in the comic tradition, are anticipated here.

The attempt to repress and then destroy the monster leads Frankenstein and his book into a landscape beyond the limits of the domestic realism toward which they had turned for succor. Such landscapes provide the spaces, distant from the centers of realistic drama, in which illicit and uncivilized extremes are acted out. The assumption of most nineteenth-century literature, from Scott forward, is that civilization was indeed advancing. The Macaulayan reading of history implied that savagery had been banished from the centers of Western experience. But in *Frankenstein*, Alps and Arctic wastes are the norm. They are the landscape of isolation from community, Victor's first obsessive choice, and they are the icons of his refusal to bring the monster in from the cold to the communal warmth of the hearth. In the cold, monster and creator enact the futility of their desires in what is almost a ritual and self-destructive parody of the Keatsian quest for the elusive fair maiden. Only Captain Walton returns, and only because he surrenders his Frankensteinian ambition. In its place, he finds an ear for the narrative in his sister, the civilized Mrs. Saville. Telling the story is made possible by the refusal to live it, and is a means to rejoin the community. His position is rather like Mary Shelley's, for she surrenders fully to her imagination, but in the writing she keeps the distance that might save her from it and deny it.

The parabolic neatness of this way of telling the story (certainly a distortion of the novel's instability and ambiguities) suggests why, for the past one hundred sixty years, it has provided metaphors for writers. The monster becomes those sexual, revolutionary, deterministic, or psychic energies that novelists and intellectuals confront even as they try to avert them. It is both rational and irrational, victim and victimizer, innocent and evil. As in the culture at large, Frankenstein and his monster keep turning up in literature—in the face of the uneducated mob in *Mary Barton*, in Magwitch's relation to Pip, his created gentleman, in the laboratories where Ursula Brangwen studies. The power of the myth of *Frankenstein* transcends the limit of the particular narrative because it is, in a way, an antimyth that has embodied in all its ambiguities the modern imagination of the potentialities and the limits of modern consciousness.

Although it takes the shape of traditional myths of the over-reacher, *Frankenstein* reverses them in ways that suggest its modernity and its kinship to the realistic impulse. In intruding secular science into a traditional Gothic framework that normally depends on supernatural machinery, Mary Shelley changes the source of the horror and mystery, and increases their credibility. They come not from evil spirits beyond the visible world, but through secular knowledge. The apparent ideal in *Frankenstein* is the recognizable domesticity that Victor Frankenstein betrays, but the novel lives far beyond the limits of this ideal. It becomes a psychomachia of the extremes of human consciousness aspiring to transcend the limits of thought and language by touching a new reality and to assert the compatibility of that reality with poetic, moral, and religious ideals.

Moreover, *Frankenstein*'s preoccupation with "creation"—though connected with literary myths and Mary Shelley's own concern with birth—is more than accidentally related to the problems and responsibilities of writing itself. Mary Shelley obviously belongs in the Romantic tradition of concern about the nature of creativity, about the relation of mind to nature, of mind to itself, and about the possibility that language—particularly poetic language—might live actively in the real world. Belonging to a literature of extremes, *Frankenstein* is nevertheless an act of rebellion against those extremes. It dramatizes, whatever its intentions, the deadliness of Shelley, her husband's, idealizing and rebellion, the consequences of Godwin, her father's, personal tyranny and his antithetic radicalism, the perversion in myths of male creativity and female dependence. In this respect, it is analogous to realism's parodic reaction to romance and to fantasies of extreme power. Like the protagonists to be disenchanted in later novels, Walton, Frankenstein, and the monster all find some radical disparity between what they read and what they experience. Each character must face the consequences of that disparity and come to terms with the limits of dream, yet the text itself is—like much realism—paradoxically Promethean. The realist novel rejects earlier fantasies of power for the limits of the probable, hoping to touch the real.

The duality is *in* the book's drama: Victor, having failed in his quest, never surrenders the dream. He is one of the first in a long tradition of fictional overreachers, of characters who seem to act out the myth of Faust in modern dress, and who transport it from the world of mystery and miracle to the commonplace. He is destroyed not by metaphysical agency—as God expelled Adam from Eden or Mephistopheles collected his share of the bargain (though echoes of these events are everywhere—but by his own nature and the consequences of living in or rejecting human community. Frankenstein is the indirect father of lesser, more humanly recognizable figures, like Becky Sharp or Pip or Lydgate, who reject the conventional limits imposed upon them by society and who are punished, more or less, for their troubles. *Frankenstein* embodies one of the central myths of realistic fiction in the nineteenth century, even in the contrast between its sensational style and its apparently explicit moral implications: a simultaneous awe and reverence toward greatness of ambition, and fear and distrust of those who act on it. Such ambivalence is almost always disguised in realistic fiction, where the manner itself seems to reject the possibility of greatness and the explicit subject is frequently the evil of aspiring to it; in Gothic fiction the energies to be suppressed by the realist ideal, by the model of Flemish painting, by worldly-wise compromise with the possible, are released. Gothic fiction, as Lowry Nelson has observed, "by its insistence on singularity and exotic setting . . . seems to have freed the minds of readers from direct involvement of their superegos and allowed them to pursue daydreams and wish fulfillment in regions where inhibitions and guilt could be suspended." The mythology of virtue rewarded, central to English realism, is to put to question in the gothic landscape where more powerful structures than social convention give shape to wish; and, as Nelson suggests, reader and writer alike were freed to pursue the possibilities of their own potential evil.

It is striking how difficult it is to locate in realistic fiction any positive and active evil. The central realist mythology is spelled out in characters like George Eliot's Tito Melema, whose wickedness is merely a gradual sliding into the consequences of a natural egoism. In Gothic fiction, but more particularly in *Frankenstein*, as Christopher Small argues, evil is both positively present and largely inexplicable. Although ostensibly based on the ideas of Godwin's rationalist ethics which see evil as a consequence of maltreatment or injustice, Frankenstein's story provides no such comfortable explanation for his own evil. Where did his decision to create the monster come from? Mere chance. Evil is a deadly and fascinating mystery whose source is in men's minds, an inexplicable but inescapable aspect of human goodness.

The transposition of the creator from God to man, the secularization of the means of creation from miracle into science, entail a transposition of the standard of moral judgment from the external world which ought to be reflecting a divine order, to the mind which is somehow forced to establish its own terms. Those terms do not fit the form of discursive or narrative explanation. *Frankenstein* is full of abrupt discontinuities and short-circuiting. The monster comes to life although Victor finds an important excuse not to reveal the fairly simple secret of life that he discovers, and it acts in the gaps of Victor's consciousness, when he is away, or feverishly and helplessly ill, or searching in the wrong place. *Frankenstein* as a text exercises its appeal in part because it fails to explain so much. The narrative has a plausibility of images, and the images themselves, not really reflective of a world divinely ordered and intelligible or susceptible to the mind, lend themselves to proliferating and unrestricted interpretations, and can be assimilated to almost any powerful mythology—especially the Freudian. But the horror of the narrative is that, like the monster, it is ultimately uncontrollable. The mind creates life, projects the landscape, but cannot control the imagined world. The landscape of the self and its texts is more frightening and dangerous than the landscape of Milton's Hell—which implies a heaven.

Literally, of course, the narrative encompasses a large part of the Northern Hemisphere, and even some of the Near East. But as it wanders across the Alps, to the northern islands of Scotland, to the frozen wastes of the Arctic, *Frankenstein* has something claustrophobic about it. The recurrence of images of ice and cold, the recurrence of patterns of family relations, the recurrence of the preoccupation with isolation and misunderstanding (Justine even admits to a crime she did not commit in order to regain a lost trust, and the gesture is, of course, suicidal): all of these give to the novel a circular and self-enclosed structure, confirmed both by the framing devices and by the ultimate reversal of pursuit. Far more, then, than a conventional realistic novel with thematic restatements, *Frankenstein* invites metaphorical reading by inviting us first to see the epic breadth as a metaphor for a narrower scope—the landscape of a single mind. In *Frankenstein*, ironically, we can see obvious intimations of later writers' attempts to throw all the action "inside." Frankenstein's very creative gesture, a thrust into a world beyond the self, is in part a projection of self upon the world. The novel, in a sense, is about the inevitability of solipsism, the alienation of the self from the world, and the necessity and desperation of the quest to rejoin it.

Some of this novel's remarkable power resides in the way its exploration of the landscape of the mind becomes a rejection of more traditional, Miltonic, ways of writing the myth, and in its preoccupation with literature it threatens to become as antiliterary as realism itself: it finds no satisfying conventions of order, power, or meaning. The monster becomes the disruption that denies any meaning to the natural except what the mind futilely thrusts upon it in the hopeless attempt to make it acquiesce in its dreams of power. The horror of the monster is, of course, its capacity for violence that results from its estrangement from both nature and social reality. That horror is most forcefully and indirectly suggested by the fact that it has no name. Violence erupts where the language fails to control by making meaning. The monster is merely a monster, "a warning," or a showing forth.

The novel's elaborate clarity of structure, Walton's tale enfolding Frankenstein's, which in turn enfolds the monster's, does not reflect a firm moral ordering, but a continuing complicating diminishment of nonverbal reality as it recedes into the distance. The language keeps reinterpreting itself, reaching for that community of understanding that allows us to posit a truth. But satisfaction does not come for any of the three protagonists. Walton would seem the ultimate judge of the experience, as the outsider, yet he explicitly accepts Frankenstein's judgment of it, and largely exculpates him by sharing his ambivalences and by rejecting his injunction to destroy the monster. The monster's own defense and explanation, lodged in the center of the story, are, however, far more convincing. This madwoman in the attic, or monster in the Alps, makes his case very sanely. Frankenstein is forced to confess his failure of responsibility to the creature, and Walton is almost persuaded, deterred only by the nonverbal fact of the monster's hideousness. In the end, however, we are left not with a judgment but with Walton's strangely uncolored report of the monster's last speech and last action. If anyone, the nameless monster has the last word; and that word expresses a longing for self-immolation and the ultimate peace in extinction: an event not narrated. Metaphorically, the Promethean spirit is the ambition to imitate reality, to make an equivalent and yet a better one. In creating the monster, Frankenstein tries to name nature and thus control it.

But he can neither name nor control. He fails to accept his creation, and this failure reflects perfectly the alienation entailed in committing himself to his imitation of nature. His first response to the monster on seeing its hideous but quite touching filial grin is to flee: "He held up the curtain of the bed; and his eyes, if eyes they may be called, were fixed on me. His jaws opened, and he muttered some inarticulate sound, while a grin wrinkled his cheeks. He might have spoken, but I did not hear; one hand was stretched out, seemingly to detain me, but I escaped, and rushed down stairs." The mind here retreats from consciousness of its own ineptitude, or from recognition of its anomalous position in nature. Like a text freed from the intentions of its author, the monster forces that author to take responsibility for him.

Composed as he is of dead bodies (and conventions), the monster is a parody of life and of forms of heroic narrative, but he is also, ironically, the embodiment of the ideal: monster *and* angel. His relation to the world is the reverse of (although it becomes the same as) that of his creator. In his obsession, Frankenstein has cut himself off from the family in which he began. In his reaction to that obsession, he cuts himself off from his creation. The monster begins without family or community and seeks what Frankenstein surrendered in creating him. Ironically, the quest for the ideal entails the loss of the saving compromises of the human condition. Implicitly, only God should undertake the responsibility of creation: "Oh! no mortal could support the horror of that countenance." Such is the traditional significance of the creation/rebellion myth. But the true sin (and the word becomes more difficult to use, the more we explore the novel) is not the Promethean theft of fire from Heaven, but the sin against self and community. It is the sin of attempting to realize the ideal; the ideal is the monstrous. This incarnate ideal dies seeking love, and his loving creator dies hating.

Nevertheless, aside from having these cosmic significances, the monster is also kin to the oppressed women and children of Victorian fiction: like Oliver Twist, Pip, Florence Dombey, and Little Nell, like Jane Eyre and Lucy Snowe, like Daniel Deronda, Henry Esmond, and Jude Fawley, the monster is an orphan, rejected by his father, uncertain of who he is or where he belongs. Naïve, well-intentioned, in danger of being led astray, he is Teufelsdröckh left in a basket, the Words-worthian child. Where in Frankenstein's story there seems no rational explanation for the entrance of evil into the world, in the monster's the explanation is clear. The monster assumes that the world makes sense somewhere beyond the limits of his knowledge, so that education seems the one thing needful. His story implies the primacy of responsi-bility to family and community, and his arguments are keenly rational, Godwinian polemics, in almost every case superior to Frankenstein's, which are ruled by vague emotions. "Yet you, my creator, detest and spurn me," cries the monster, "to whom thou art bound by ties only dissoluble by the annihilation of one of us. You purpose to kill me. How dare you sport thus with life?" Amid all the extraordinary reversals in this novel, perhaps the most startling is the way the monster becomes, in the dramatized action, the intellectual and moral superior of his creator. He is the aspiration for meaning in reality, thwarted by the injustice experience teaches; he is thus kin to the dreamers of Victorian dreams who are doomed to disenchantment: he is another anomaly, the true image of their perceived deviance into impossible romantic dreams. The audacity of a murderer accusing his creator of "sporting with life"!

"Make me happy, and I shall again be virtuous," he pleads. The point is a political one, and much of the monster's experience is used as an exemplar of the Godwinian view that evil enters the spirit as a result of the injustice of others. Man is born naturally good, and there is every evidence that the monster's heart is in the right place (after all, it was put there by Frankenstein). The monster represents a kind of Dickensian reading (almost Carlylean, but that Carlyle could not be-lieve in man's natural goodness) of the French Revolution. Abused, abandoned, maltreated, deprived, he turns, unlike good Victorian chil-dren, in vengeance on his master and his master's world.

But none of the characters comfortable in domestic harmony can believe that the world is governed unjustly until the monster strikes. Such blindness makes it evident that domesticity is a deliberately built defense against the disruptive norm of disaster. This is true even for the monster, who enjoys domestic bliss only by peering in the De Laceys' window. When Elizabeth weeps for Justine before the hang-ing, she is comforted by Frankenstein's father, who says, "If she is, as you believe, innocent, rely on the justice of our law." But in realistic fiction, experience brings knowledge and disenchantment, and one of the novel's themes is an anti-Miltonic version of the danger of knowledge. Disenchantment, a recognition of one's own limits, of the injustice pervasive in society, and of the power of society over one's own ambitions, here is afforded no divine relief. While the characteristic realistic protagonist ends in some sort of compromise, usually eased by marriage to an attractive counterpart, *Frankenstein*, working in a different mode, does not allow secular wisdom and moderation. It deals with the motif of knowledge and innocence and disenchantment on a scale far larger than that of the conventional *Bildungsroman*. Frankenstein's quest for knowledge can be seen as a dramatic metaphor for the universal ambition that leads to lost innocence. It is not merely Frankenstein in this novel who becomes disenchanted: each major character learns something of the nature of his own illusions. As the reality of death (which is really the product of Frankenstein's knowledge) enters the almost idyllic household of Frankenstein's family, the romance of domestic harmony gives way to a deep gloom. What happens to Frankenstein in his pursuit of knowledge happens, inescapably, to everyone no matter how apparently safe or good.

Frankenstein points the Faustian moral to Walton: "Learn from me, if not by my precepts, at least by my example, how dangerous is the acquirement of knowledge, and how much happier that man is who believes his native town to be the world, than he who aspires to become greater than his nature will allow." But this moral— particularly appropriate to the realistic novel—is argued very ambivalently. Even the monster repeats the argument (as he must, being Frankenstein's alter ego): "Increase of knowledge only discovered to me more clearly what a wretched outcast I was." As his knowledge grows, he cries out: "Oh, that I had for ever remained in my native wood, nor known nor felt beyond the sensation of hunger, thirst, and heat!" Yet Mary Shelley knows, as the monster learned, that there is no returning to innocence; the rhetoric implies that the innocence is a lie, and that the disaster that follows its loss is as inevitable as the loss itself. "Of what a strange nature is knowledge! It clings to the mind, when it has once seized on it, like a lichen on the rock. I wished sometimes to shake off all thought and feeling; but I learned that there was but one means to overcome the sensation of pain, and that was death." The monster knows that only silence ends the disparity between word and life. Frankenstein, however, cannot give up the quest or insist unambiguously on the moral of his story. His last speech is a masterpiece of doubt: "Farewell, Walton!" he says. "Seek happiness in tranquillity, and avoid ambition, even if it be only the apparently innocent one of distinguishing yourself in science and discoveries. Yet why do I say this? I have myself been blasted in these hopes, yet another may succeed." Death is the only resolution, and yet it resolves nothing since knowledge and innocence are continuing aspects of human experience. The tension worked out in *Frankenstein* between ambition and natural harmony, as between creator and creature, mind and reality, is not resolved.

This tension is central to realism which, in its parodic and ironic modes, seems sometimes to lend its conventions to the making of an immense cautionary fable, but just as often dramatically belies the fable. Not Frankenstein's cool abstract language and logical balancing of sentences:

> During these last days I have been occupied in examining my past conduct; nor do I find it blameable. In a fit of enthusiastic madness I created a rational creature, and was bound towards him, to assure, as far as was in my power, his happiness and well-being. This was my duty; but there was another still paramount to that. My duties towards the beings of my own species had greater claims to my attention, because they included a greater proportion of happiness or misery.

Frankenstein stands here at a kind of Olympian distance from his experience. He manages to achieve the hero's absolution from responsibility (at least for this moment) by accepting an intolerable dualism. The responsibility to the self's largest desires (its enthusiastic madness) is incompatible with the responsibility to family and society. Any moral calculus reveals an irrational world—one incompatible with the self, and hence unjust and incoherent. Against this sort of dualism the realist novel builds its defenses through the structures of compromise: excess and ambition must be excluded; the prose must be less calculating and abstract, deferring to the flexibility and casualness and un-ideality of the quotidian. Realism thus becomes capable of opening new, more fluid, and unstable imaginations of experience, finding more various—if disguised—articulations of desire, while at the same time establishing that distance between desire and experience, language and object, that allows narrative to serve equally as a retreat from experience.

Frankenstein enacts an impasse: the horror of going ahead and the emptiness of return. By providing an image of satisfied desire, it provides a metaphor for the price of heroism. If heroism is personal satisfaction writ large, it is also monstrous. For that desire turns out to be an unnameable projection of self onto the world rejected in order to satisfy it. In attaining the desire one loses it, for it destroys the possibility of contact with another and thus ends by destroying the self. Alternatively, the refusal to act out the desire is a refusal to test the limits of the self. Walton at the end is trapped within the prison of social limits.

This leads to one final point about Frankenstein as a hero, and as a type of the realist hero. His unattractiveness to the reader follows from three qualities. The first is precisely his obsession with great action. As he is obsessed he is also, necessarily, cruel. Like the author of any narrative, he must exclude, shape, turn secondary characters into waste. He turns away from his responsibilities; it is with a new sense of these responsibilities that he dies. The second is that he is really unequal to his own ambitions. He has the technical power to create life, but he has not the moral power to cope with his technique. In this respect, he is rather like Dostoyevski's Raskolnikov although he is treated without the psychological intimacy that makes us participate in Raskolnikov's weaknesses. But the third is more central to my immediate concern here. It is the nature of his behavior when he undergoes one of his regular spasms of desire to return to the virtues of domesticity, "the amiableness of domestic affection." On these occasions, Frankenstein is the passive hero.

If ambition is evil, then, one might think, the absence of ambition is virtue. And it is one of the curious facts about the most virtuous heroes and heroines of nineteenth-century English realist fiction that they are inefficacious, inactive people. Their fullest energies are expended only (if at all) in response to external threat, in the preservation of familial and communal ties. Like Dorothea Brooke and Daniel Deronda, they are somehow incapable of imagining a satisfying action, a way of life which will allow them seriously to act at all. Alexander Welsh has studied in detail the nature of Scott's strangely passive hero, and his analysis of the reasons for that passivity are to the point in considering Frankenstein's actions. For one thing, Scott's characters and his novels are imprisoned, like Walton, by an ideal of prudence, and not a calculating prudence: "A prudent hero who cannot be deliberately prudent can have no active role. He can do no deeds of violence; nor can he survive by cunning. He is wholly at the mercy of

the forces that surround him, and thus acted upon rather than acting"
[*The Hero of the Waverley Novels*]. We recognize something of this both
in Frankenstein's commitment to natural feeling (which excludes calcu-
lation until the deathbed) and in his persistent blaming of cruel Fate for
his difficulties. But, as Welsh points out, "the passive hero only
partially admits of a rational explanation." The passive hero, he says, is
not neutral, but committed to the ideals—the prudence and superiority—
of civilized society. He becomes an observer, then, "committed to the
civil state, and observes the uncivil." The application of all this to
Frankenstein is striking. As an ambitious hero, he wants to improve
things, and in much of the novel, as I have pointed out, the mecha-
nisms of society are regarded as cruel and unjust. But the notion of
domestic affections and the needs for communal and family ties run
deep. As Frankenstein longs for these, his ambition drops away and he
falls into inaction. The whole narrative reveals that Frankenstein, as an
active figure, does only two things: he acts obsessively in creating the
monster (and it should be noted that even here he insists on his
passivity before fate—this provides the moral excuse); and at the end,
he acts obsessively (and ineffectually) in pursuing him. The passivity is
most painful when he retreats from recognition of the evil he has
created and allows Justine to die. But his initial flight from the monster
is also a supreme passive act: if you don't see it, it's not there, as Jack
Burden says in *All the King's Men*. After he flees from the aborted
attempt to create a mate for the monster, he glides into one of the
scenes that will become typical of Victorian fiction. He finds himself
on a boat which drifts beyond his control in a storm, and he comes
ashore at precisely the place where the monster has just killed Clerval.
His response is to fall into one of his characteristic illnesses that return
him to the helplessness of infancy and to the care of his father and
family. In other words, the passivity of this hero is to be explained not
only by the ideals of prudence and domestic harmony and natural
affection, or by the ideal of the civilized community, but by the
irrational need to escape the consequences of adulthood, to retreat to
the innocence and helplessness of the womb where the heroic expression of selfhood is denied and replaced by the comfort of dependence
and the absorption of love of others. Narratively, it is a retreat from
the shaping energies of imagination.

Thus *Frankenstein* provides us with a hero whose being expresses
precisely those tensions that will preoccupy later English novelists.
Frankenstein enacts not only the role of the realist hero but the alternatives

to that role which do much to explain the characteristic shape of realist fiction. The failure of Frankenstein to destroy his knowledge and to retreat to innocence foreshadows, I think, the ultimate self-destruction of realist techniques. Of course, this is a dangerously oversimple generalization, and puts rather a heavy burden on a novel which makes no such claims. But studying *Frankenstein* can help us to understand some of the powerful and inexplicit energies that lie beneath the surface of realist fiction in England and can help explain both the pervasive resistance to and distrust of ambition and energy in its heroes—their strange dulness and inadequacy—and the rebellion against a stifling society, the equally strange and subversive fascination with ambition and evil energies. Who would prefer Amelia Sedley to Becky Sharp, or Little Nell to Quilp, or Daniel Deronda to Grandcourt? The irrational and rebellious are latent in every important English realist novel, and within every hero or heroine there is a Frankenstein—or his monster—waiting to get out. The hero carries the narrative's burden of creation.

Frankenstein: Creation as Catastrophe

Paul Sherwin

As *Frankenstein* gets under way, we are lured by the promise of a new beginning: Walton's pathbreaking journey to the North Pole. Bound for Archangel to assemble a crew, Walton is inspired by the cold northern wind to envision a perpetually warm and radiant paradise at the summit of the globe. To be there would be to capture the heavens in a glance, to tap earth's central power source, and to stand within the magic circle of the poets he once sought to emulate but whose sublimity he could not match. Such extravagance is easier to credit if we keep in mind the uneasiness it is intended to dispel: "There is something at work in my soul, which I do not understand." Perhaps for his own good, and certainly at the dramatically right moment, the quest founders somewhere in the frozen wastes between Archangel and the Pole, just where Walton is waylaid by Frankenstein, who is feverishly pursuing the path of the Creature's departure. It may be more accurate to say that the quest is deflected. For although Walton is relegated to the periphery of the fiction, ushering in and out a wondrous tale that preempts his own, he is profoundly implicated as well. The tale, of course, is a monitory example meant for him, but it is also a riddle of fate that means him: the mystery that he is and that becomes his by virtue of his fascinated participation in Frankenstein's story. In short, Walton is in the critical position, and nowhere is his situation better evidenced than at the end of the novel. Frankenstein, burdened by his tale's monstrous residue, concludes his narrative by enjoining Walton

From *PMLA* 96, no. 5 (October 1981). © 1981 by the Modern Language Association of America.

to slay the Creature after his death. Yet the climactic encounter with the Creature unsettles everything even more and leaves Walton powerless to act. The final word and deed belong to the Creature, who vows to undo the scene of his creation once he bounds from the ship: "I shall . . . seek the most northern extremity of the globe; I shall collect my funeral pile, and consume to ashes this miserable frame, that its remains may afford no light . . . my ashes will be swept into the sea by the winds." To Walton, however, belongs the burden of the mystery as he watches this self-destroying artifact vanish into darkness and distance and contemplates a catastrophe at the Pole.

I

Mary Shelley might well have titled her novel *One Catastrophe after Another*. For Frankenstein, who is dubiously in love with his own polymorphously disastrous history, the fateful event to which every other catastrophe is prelude or postscript is the creation. According to the archaic model implicit in his narrative, transcendence is equivalent to transgression, and his presumptuous deed is invested with the aura of a primal sin against nature that somehow justifies the ensuing retributive bother. Condemned by nature's gods to limitless suffering, the aspiring hero learns his properly limited human place. *Frankenstein*, however, knows differently. A reading alert to the anti-Gothic novel Mary Shelley inscribes within her Gothic tale will discover that nothing is simple or single. *The* critical event is impossible to localize, terms such as "justice" and "injustice" do not so much mean as undergo vicissitudes of meaning, and all the narrators are dispossessed of their authority over the text. As the central misreader, Frankenstein is the chief victim of the text's irony, the humor becoming particularly cruel whenever he thinks he is addressing the supernatural powers that oversee his destiny, for his invocatory ravings never fail to conjure up his own Creature. Indeed, the evacuation of spiritual presence from the world of the novel suggests that *Frankenstein* is more a house in ruins than the house divided that its best recent critics have shown it to be. The specter of deconstruction rises: doubtless future interpreters will describe a text that compulsively subverts its own performance and that substitutes for its missing center the senseless power play of a catastrophic Gothic machine. Yet the Gothic is always already demystified, the ruin of an anterior world of large spiritual forces and transcendent desires that the most relentless of demystifiers cannot will away. *Frankenstein*, although arguably a Gothic fiction, remains a living novel because it is a haunted house, ensouled by the anxious spirit that perturbs all belated romances.

While the unconsummated spirit raised by *Frankenstein* cannot be put to rest, one might suppose that *das Unheimliche* can be contained within the spacious edifice of Freudian psychoanalysis. Freud's antithetical system provides an interpretive context for many of the anomalies disclosed by an ironic reading: the dissonance of overt and implicit meanings, the obscure sense of having trespassed on sacred ground, the appalling secret that craves expression yet must be protected as though it were a holy thing. In addition, the novel's catastrophic model functions in a way strikingly similar to the Freudian psychic apparatus. Instead of hubris, there is the drive's excess; instead of a downcast hero assaulted by phantasmagoria, there is the boundless anxiety occasioned by the proliferation of repressed desire; and instead of the restrictive gods, there is the exalted secondary process, intended to keep the apparatus stable by binding or incarcerating mobile energy. More telling, the catastrophic model is an almost exact duplicate of the oedipal scenario, the most privileged psychoanalytic thematic and the dynamic source of Freud's mature topography of the psyche. The way is opened for a recentering of the novel's unresolved intellectual and emotional turmoil.

Of course, the Freudian way has increasingly become, and always was, a wildly extravagant detour or series of detours, and staking out a position in the psychoanalytic field can be as agonizing as "choosing" a neurosis. Still, when one reads that Walton is about to enact the favorite dream of his youth, seeking a passage through the ice to the warm Pole, where he may "discover the wondrous power which attracts the needle," or that Frankenstein struggles "with a child's blindness" to break through "the fortifications and impediments that seemed to keep human beings from entering the citadel of nature," it is hard not to translate such statements into the formulations of a recognizably classical psychoanalysis. I should acknowledge here that I am averse to reducing the questing drive in *Frankenstein* to a desire for primordial union with, or active possession of, the maternal body and that I think it is a dangerous critical error to conceive the novel as a tale told by an idiot, signifying. I do, however, consider the orthodox Freudian approach a formidable antagonist to the sort of psychoanalytic interpretation I venture in the second section of this essay; and I should like to sketch my own "Freudian" romancing of *Frankenstein*, before proceeding to unweave it, in part because none of the many analytic runs at the text in recent years seems to me as persuasive as it might be and in part because something in me is deeply responsive to such a reading. Psychoanalysis, it may be said, is properly attuned to an important element in the life of the mind; its problem is that it fancies that part the whole.

A reading of the oedipal drama the novel reenacts can begin with a notice of the first overt catastrophe recorded in Frankenstein's narrative: his witnessing, at fifteen, the terrible power of a lightning bolt during a thunderstorm. When the adult Frankenstein describes the event, which occurred at a time when his enthusiasm for alchemy had redoubled the urgency of his endeavors to penetrate nature's secrets, his excited rhetoric betrays the insistent presence of a forgotten childhood scene. "I remained, while the storm lasted, watching its progress with curiosity and delight. As I stood at the door, on a sudden I beheld a stream of fire issue from an old and beautiful oak . . . and so soon as the dazzling light vanished the oak had disappeared, and nothing remained but a blasted stump." In the original version of the text it is the father who discourses on the nature of lightning and who controls the symbolically castrating bolt that cripples desire: "he constructed a small electrical machine, and exhibited a few experiments . . . which drew down that fluid from the clouds." The son is, as it were, shocked into the latency stage; a sudden influx of self-revulsion impels him to denounce "natural history and all its progeny as a deformed and abortive creation . . . which could never even step within the threshold of real knowledge . . . an unusual tranquility and gladness of soul . . . followed the relinquishing of my ancient and latterly tormenting studies."

The next critical event in Frankenstein's history is his mother's death, and a period of mourning delays his departure for the university. Once there, he abruptly resumes his former studies, reconverted by Professor Waldman's panegyric on modern chemists: "these philosophers . . . penetrate into the recesses of nature. . . . They ascend into the heavens . . . they can command the thunders of heaven." The difficult work of mourning—the guilt-ridden withdrawal of attachment to the mother, a process allied to the transferal of Frankenstein's love to Elizabeth and his decision to leave home—is undone. Waldman's vision of the master who can refind the lost object and command limitless power has the characteristically unsettling impact of a pubescent irruption of libido, and the idea of the mother, set free by death for fantasy elaboration, becomes the focus of the regressive descent into phantasmagoria that constitutes Frankenstein's reanimation project. Within the secretive darkness of vaults and charnels, he dabbles in filth, his heart sickening at the work of his hands as he disturbs, "with profane fingers, the tremendous secrets of the human frame." The imagery has an unmistakably anal and masturbatory cast. At once feces and phallus, the filth is also the maternal presence he is assembling from phantasmal body parts and buried wishes. In sum, Frankenstein's descent is a grotesque act of lovemaking, the son stealing into the womb that bore him in order to implant his seed. Having fully re-membered the form of his desire, the mother restored by a far more radical rescue than the one by which the father claimed her, he is ready to draw rebellious Promethean fire down from the heavens and realize his grandiose conception, the creation proper.

Or so Frankenstein dreams: the time never can be right for this obsessional neurotic:

> With an anxiety that almost amounted to agony, I collected the instruments of life around me, that I might infuse a spark of being into the lifeless thing that lay at my feet . . . My candle was nearly burnt out, when . . . I saw the dull yellow eye of the creature open, and a convulsive motion agitated its limbs. How can I describe my emotions at this catastrophe . . . ?

What is most strange here is that the Creature is a sleeping beauty until its orgasmic stirring rouses Frankenstein to recognize the monstrosity before him. We confront the antithetical aspects not only of the fantasy mother but of the son's desire. The Creature is thus a befouled version of the son who would usurp the father's prerogatives, the would-be transcendent father of himself who now beholds the squalor of his actual origins and wishes. But such an interpretation is still oversimplified. The scene scatters the self into every possible familial position; the Creature, on the contrary, is a massively overdetermined representation of the entire scene as well as of the related Oedipus complex. We can infer that the Creature also embodies the fantasy father because it is as much a ubiquitous gaze under which Frankenstein cowers as a nightmare image that bewilders his sight. The convulsive agitation of the aroused Creature suggests ejaculation; yet although this "filthy mass" represents a monstrously oversized phallus, its dread-provoking *corps morcelé* bears the stigma of castration, calling to mind the Lacanian castrated phallus. This difficulty can be resolved if the Creature is viewed as Frankenstein's renounced phallic self, the self he yields to the father, perhaps detached in the very achievement of orgasm, at once the moment of the organ's autonomy and a repetition of the father's act of begetting. Whatever the interpretation, when Frankenstein mimics the Creature's convulsions after his flight and subsequent nightmare, the appropriate description, given his regressed condition, is anal evacuation, which Freud claims is the child's typical response to the primal scene. Here we may note that Mary Shelley writes in the introduction of "the working of some powerful engine," but Frankenstein has a spark, not a bolt, and as he begins to infuse life, his candle has dwindled. Already defeated by his own scene of origins, Frankenstein is barred from the compensatory replay he intends. Instead the creation precipitously repeats the occasion of his mental trouble, the traumatic fixation he is fated to suffer again and again.

It is not until several chapters later and some two years after the creation that the novel, approaching another dangerous crossing, is disturbed into strength. By now the abandoned or liberated Creature has embarked on its career of murderous inroads into Frankenstein's family romance, and the creator, increasingly abandoned to morbid anxiety, gravitates to the Alps, whose "savage and enduring scenes" become the stage for an attempted reworking of his defining scene. Alternately plunging and mounting for three days, he is at last urged to penetrate the mists rising like incense from the ravine of Arve toward the surrounding heights, coming to a halt in a spectacular setting where "a power mighty as Omnipotence" manifests itself. As in the lightning scene of his youth, he stands apart, gazing ecstatically. From the recess of a rock, he looks across the troubled surface of *La Mer de Glace*, the glacier poured down from the summits in an eternally solemn procession, and in the distance the stupendous bright dome of Mont Blanc rises "in awful majesty" before him. Power, throughout this section of the novel, is envisioned as the power to wound: "the . . . silence of this glorious presence-chamber of imperial Nature was broken . . . by . . . the cracking . . . of the accumulated ice, which, through the silent working of immutable laws, was ever and anon rent and torn, as if it had been but a plaything." To be where Power is would mean to be above the turmoil of desire, the desire of and for the mother (*la mère*), whom the father controls and possesses by right. Restaging his primal-scene fantasy under the gaze of the terrific god of the Alps, Frankenstein has a dual aim. While he would seem to be propitiating the father, submitting to the law that freezes or castrates desire, he may also be seeking a way out of his oedipal impasse by identifying with a transcendent paternal principle that enables the son, in his turn, to put on the power of the father.

The scene dissipates when Frankenstein's call to the "wandering spirits" of his mountain god summons the Creature, his own errant spirit. Rising up to demand a mate from *his* father, the Creature forces Frankenstein into the unamiable role of a jealously restrictive frustrate father, a lame parody of his dread paternal imago. A possible explanation for this failed oedipal normalization is that the excessive harshness of the agency whose function is to suppress the complex actually reinforces Frankenstein's most primitive longings. But such an overweening superego is too deeply contaminated by unregenerate desire to be construed as autonomous. Rather, it is a phantasmic derivative of the complex, a shadowy type of that relentless internal danger which the Creature consummately represents. At least the Creature is almost a representation. Though actualized in the world of the fiction, out of narrative necessity, the Creature is so uncannily fearful that it cannot in fact be seen. Yet how is one to comprehend a representation that transcends representation, that is apparently the thing itself? Frankenstein's astonishing psychic achievement, in Freudian terms, is the construction of a primal repression, whose constitutive role in psychic development is to structure the unconscious as an articulate erotogenic zone. His sorrow is that this catastrophically global repression, or rerepression, is so radically alienated from the ego that it disqualifies any attempt at integration, insistently transmitting its full affective charge and thus preventing the institution of a firm psychic apparatus.

The developing plot of the novel elaborates the grim psychic consequences of Frankenstein's deepening subjugation to his dark double. The Creature is cast as the active partner in what amounts to a bizarre conspiracy, rehearsing in another register the scandalous history of the creator's desire, with Frankenstein bound to what Melanie Klein calls the "depressive position." As a recognizable human world recedes and the Creature becomes a progressively more enthralling superpower, Frankenstein joins in the frenetic dance of death that impels these mutually fascinated antagonists across the waste places of the earth. By now wholly the Creature's creature, he must be considered a florid psychotic, pursuing the naked form of his desire in a fantastic nowhere that is his own. Of course, the consummating thrust of the sword eludes Frankenstein, who is drained by his interminable quest, but the Creature, that monstrous embodiment of his unremitting parental nightmare, can say "I am satisfied."

I am not, nor in fact is the Creature, though admittedly the coherence and audacity of this psychoanalytic reading give it considerable authority. While it is true that by the end of Frankenstein's narrative creator and Creature form a kind of symbiotic unit whose significance various orthodox analytic schools are well suited to explain, such pathological relatedness can be as cogently elucidated by Hegel's master-slave dialectic or by its derivatives in Lacan and Girard. This fearful symmetry, moreover, stems largely from a perverse misreading that Frankenstein sets in motion and that the traditional psychoanalytic critic refines on.

Consider a privileged psychoanalytic moment in the text, Frankenstein's nightmare after the creation and his subsequent response:

> I thought I saw Elizabeth, in the bloom of health, walking
> in the streets. . . . Delighted and surprised, I embraced her;
> but as I imprinted the first kiss on her lips, they became
> livid with the hue of death; her features appeared to change,
> and I thought that I held the corpse of my dead mother in
> my arms; a shroud enveloped her form, and I saw the
> grave-worms crawling in the folds of the flannel. I started
> from my sleep with horror . . . every limb became con-
> vulsed: when, by the dim and yellow light of the moon . . .
> I beheld . . . the miserable monster whom I had created. He
> held up the curtain of the bed; and his eyes, if eyes they may
> be called, were fixed on me. His jaws opened, and he
> muttered some inarticulate sounds, while a grin wrinkled his
> cheeks. He might have spoken, but I did not hear, one hand
> was stretched out, seemingly to detain me, but I escaped.
> . . . I took refuge in the courtyard . . . fearing each sound as
> if it were to announce the approach of the demoniacal corpse.
> . . . A mummy again endued with animation could not be
> so hideous.

Restricting the interpretive game to a psychoanalytic strategy and overlooking those automatic signals (Elizabeth as streetwalker, the mummy-mommy pun) with which a prevalent mode of subcriticism clutters the mind, what can we deduce from the passage? Most simply, there is a treacherous wishing-dreading circuit that links Elizabeth and the Creature to the mother, the central term of the triad. As symbolic counter, Elizabeth is the mother's corpse, and in embracing this cousin-sister-bride Frankenstein reaches through her to take hold of the maternal body he intends to possess. The hungry phallic worms only faintly disguise his wish, and when it comes too close to fulfillment he wakens excitedly on the bed of his desire, where he is confronted by the Creature as demoniacal corpse, its negativity a token of the repression that distorts the wish even in the dream. Once this basic fantasy material is unearthed, numerous variations on the dream scenario are possible: Elizabeth is killed off because she tempts Frankenstein to a sublimated version of his true desire; Frankenstein's lust is overwhelmed by his fear of being sucked into the cloaca of the vampirish mother; and the Creature is alternatively or simultaneously the accusatory phallic father, the rephallicized mother, and (in view of the multiplication of genital symbols in the dream) the castrated self.

At issue is where and how closely such a commentary touches the passage. Clearly a psychoanalytic reading is attuned to Frankenstein's anxious, conflict-ridden experience, but the bewilderment of his desire and his relationships is at most tangentially allied to sexuality and not at all to incest, which is a poor trope for the disturbing center of the dream. To reopen the text we must reverse the process by which the analyst translates the teasingly idiomatic world of the dream into a too familiar context of anticipated meanings. At the outset we need to recall that Frankenstein has devoted two years to his animation project; that, aside from a few detours into the abyss, he has been soaring in a rarefied atmosphere where it is impossible to breathe; and that now he is responding to the dissolution of his hopes as well as to the embarrassing fact of the Creature, a singular enormity for which there is no place in his experiential horizon. His response is revealing: first literal flight, then flight into sleep, and finally flight from both the dream and the Creature. The dream itself, the way it is lived, beautifully testifies to the disorienting shock of Frankenstein's reentry into reality. The dreamer does not know what is happening to him. He exists discontinuously, overwhelmed by sudden, appalling contrasts and baffled by the uncertain boundaries between the real and the phantasmal. When the imagery of the dream's core, derived from the creator's descent into the house of the dead, is brought together with the family world he bracketed during the creation, the most canny (*heimlich*) of worlds, the effect is peculiarly poignant. Elizabeth is present because she is a fit emblem of the dream of loveliness that has slipped away from him, and the mother is there mainly because she is the only dead person

[margin annotation: counter idea]

who matters to him. Waking, within the dream, into emptiness and worse, Frankenstein beholds the idealized form of his mother, preserved intact by his memory as by the shroud in the dream, falling prey to anonymous malforming powers. He has nothing to hold onto except the body of death, and as he wakens he spills out of one nightmare into another, finding himself face to face with the abomination he has created.

For Frankenstein there is an inescapable connection between the intruding "grave-worms" of the dream and the monster that invades his curtained bed. Only after the Creature's narrative cuts into his and compels us to reread the passage do we appreciate how mistaken Frankenstein is. He will not hear and cannot see. Reading a sinister intention into this newborn's clumsy gestures, he is terrified by a shadow of his own casting, a bad interpretation that climaxes all the traumatic events and that irrevocably determines the creation as the Bad Event. The process of misreading is most clearly exemplified when he next encounters the Creature, during a nocturnal storm in the Alps. The figure is suddenly illuminated by a bolt of lightning. A series of staccato flashes enables Frankenstein to make out the Creature's dizzying course as it leaps from crag to crag, and in the intervals of darkness, while his eye is recovering from each blinding glance, he reflects. None but this "devil" could have strangled his little brother or framed the saintly Justine for the murder. "No sooner did that idea cross my imagination, than I became convinced of its truth." Unlike those who convict Justine on the basis of mere appearance, Frankenstein has the facts right, but his imputation of diabolical designs to the Creature is a gross distortion, as is his summary judgment, which marks him as the prototypical psychoanalytic reader of his own text: "I conceived the being . . . in the light of my own vampire, my own spirit let loose from the grave, and forced to destroy all that was dear to me." The proper analytic rejoinder is that Frankenstein is an overreacting, moralizing misreader, rather like the self-blinded ego that travesties the id. The analogy is admissible, however, only if it is restricted to an illustrative function. Reading it literally, the critic perpetuates Frankenstein's interpretive error, violating the Creature's spiritual integrity and evading the aesthetic problem this figure poses.

The overriding ironies are that it is the psychoanalytic reader, not the Creature, who reenacts the history of Frankenstein's desire in another register and that what enables the analyst to articulate this desire so persuasively is what discredits the interpretation. Both protagonist and critic are family obsessed (or, rather, preoccupied with that aspect of the familial which is an adjunct to the personal), backward-looking, fatalistic, fixated on a terrible secret. They exist within the same disturbed conceptual horizon, conceiving experience and the experiential universe in solipsistic terms. Once again the alchemist is reborn in the scientist: the projector would look or crash through the phenomenal to an occult, transcendent reality. An apparent difference is that while Frankenstein, who is by turns indifferent to and sickened by appearances, views reality as the elixir that will grant him power over things, the analyst sees appearances, no matter how superficially hideous, as a deceptively appealing screen and reality as a squalor. Yet that squalor is the critic's secret of secrets, the means of pouring the light of meaning into the dark world of desire and so of overpowering the text. For both, however, the act of knowledge is as devastating for knower and known as the attempt to "sieze the inmost Form" in Blake's "The Crystal Cabinet." The image—world or text—shatters, and one is left holding onto a corpse. That form of alienation, for the orthodox psychoanalytic critic, is the literal, dead letter of the Freudian corpus, the petrified formulations of an introjected mystery religion that are interposed as a barrier between reader and text. But such "repression" of the text results in a solution that merely replays an element in the text, its most conventional, superficial, or manifest dimension: that of Gothic melodrama. In this intense, simplistically dualistic world of obsessional neurosis, the analyst discovers truth.

One thinks of the novel's melodramatic climax, the Creature's ravishment of the bride on Frankenstein's wedding night: if any literary work can be opened up by a psychoanalytic approach, this incident suggests that *Frankenstein* must be the text. Reflecting "how fearful the combat which I momentarily expected would be to my wife," Frankenstein bids Elizabeth retire to the bridal chamber while he paces restlessly through the house in anticipation of the Creature's advent. Roused by a scream, he rushes in to find her limp body thrown across the bed, when, through the open casement, he beholds his monstrous rival: "he seemed to jeer as with his fiendish finger he pointed towards the corpse. . . . I rushed towards the window and, drawing a pistol from my bosom, fired; but he eluded me . . . and, running with the swiftness of lightning, plunged into the lake." However polymorphously perverse an analytic rendering of the incident, I would not seriously dispute its applicability to Frankenstein, whose evocation the reading is based on, though it could be claimed that an exposition of his sexual trouble merely brings one to the horizon of a larger spiritual problem. But how apposite is such a commentary to Elizabeth? Where the analyst would place sexuality, for her there is a void. As for the Creature, he is not, at this point, sexless, his desire having become eroticized because his hideousness limits him to spying on the women of the De Lacey household and to gazing on the loveliness of Frankenstein's mother and Justine in the aesthetically distanced form of a portrait or a sleeping body. Unless Elizabeth somehow means these images, it is hard to understand why she should matter to the Creature. Frankenstein does matter to him, however—certainly not because of some repressed homosexual attachment and not because Frankenstein is the Lacanian or Girardian "other" who confers value on the object of (the other's) desire. What, then, does the Creature want from Frankenstein? He seeks reparation for his sorrows, and to this end he attempts to engage Frankenstein in dialogue, again not because Frankenstein is the Lacanian "Other" whose recognition is all he really wants but because Frankenstein alone can provide a suitable mate with whom to share his enforced solitude. After Frankenstein breaks his word, mangling the half-finished monsteress in full view of the Creature, the Creature keeps his. The killing of Elizabeth is at once a way of establishing a relationship with the only human being to whom he can claim kinship and a desperately antierotic act designed to teach his creator what he suffers. The Creature's murderous career, an ingenious counterplot, compels Frankenstein to read what amounts to a Freudian text in reality.

The foregoing may seems not only naïvely overliteral but sentimental. Am I not resorting to "pernicious casuistry" (Shelley), excusing the Creature because he is an "exception," and how can I justly argue that his truth is intersubjectivity when his only contacts are hypothetical? In dealing with the Creature one needs to exercise the hesitancy such questions induce; that is, the critic should, insofar as possible, respect the text. When J. M. Hill, a psychoanalytic adept, claims that the Creature "cannot fathom the depths of passion which urge vengeance" and when a generally skeptical George Levine remarks that the Creature "doesn't fully understand the power of irrational energies which he himself enacts," they are presumably thinking about the unconscious of the unconscious, whatever that means, but I am fairly sure these are not critical statements. Despite appearances, the Creature remains a scandal for analytic readers because he does not fit Freud's specifications: his unpresentable outside (only apparently idlike) balks (but not purposefully, as in Freudian repression) his un-ambiguously presentable inside. Of course, given the sophisticated rhetorical techniques of the psychoanalytic arsenal, there is nothing to prevent critics from remaking the Creature in whatever image they wish, from transforming any presence into an absence or any absence into a presence, as they see fit. Critics can thereby preserve the coherence of a reading, but in so doing they sacrifice too much. For the Creature's story is something finer than just another version of, or a sentimental recoil from, Frankenstein's, and the Creature himself is *Frankenstein*'s great, original turn on tradition, a disturbingly uncanny literal figuration that ought to rouse the critical faculties to act.

An editor of a recent collection of essays on *Frankenstein* [George Levine] observes, "So pervasive has been the recognition that the Monster and Frankenstein are two aspects of the same being that the writers in this volume assume rather than argue it." Among the powerful forces responsible for collapsing the two into one is the inertial drift of both reading and textuality, fostered here by the mystifying allure of those grand figures of thought, doubling and monsterism. Within us there is also a need, perhaps a compulsion, to return things to an originative, determining source, especially when the human producer of an object or act is involved. This exigency is manifest in forms ranging from the ghoulish rage of Shelley's Count Cenci, who would reappropriate a "particle of my divided being" by raping his daughter, to the comparatively mild critical reduction of the Creature to the dark complement of Frankenstein's light or of creator and created to epiphenomena of some larger whole, be it Blake's inconceivable unfallen Albion, Mary Shelley's psyche, or the Freudian psychic apparatus. At this stage of *Frankenstein* criticism, the motif of the double can be useful only if it sharpens awareness of the irreducibly complex otherness intrinsic to the self or of the Creature as an autonomous "other self" duplicitously representing the traditional alter ego. Even supposing that the Creature owes his engenderment to Frankenstein's oedipal scene, he is no more reducible to it than any of us is to what our parents happened to be thinking when they conceived us. How different from Frankenstein's is the Creature's recurrent catastrophic scene of rejection and exclusion. The Creature's utmost desire is that another reciprocate his need for sympathetic relationship, and even after he becomes searingly conscious of his exclusion from the human community and begins to objectify the negativity he arouses in others, we recognize that his aggression is a by-product of disintegration, not an innate drive that has been cathartically unbound. If, with a reader's ideal blindness, we can hear the bereavement of the Creature's whole self, we recognize too that he looks back at us with "speculative eyes." Freed, by the end, from his creator's self-consuming rage, he makes his destiny his choice, emblazoning himself as a giant form of Solitude, an existence made absolute by its confinement to the hell of being itself.

Still, the Creature's fate is to be misread, and any thematic capture necessarily restricts, however much it restitutes. In a moment of remarkable self-awareness he reflects that if he had been introduced to humanity not by the patriarchal De Laceys but "by a young soldier, burning for glory and slaughter," he would "have been imbued with different sensations." His history, then, is only a possible actualization of his essence, which is to say that the Creature's principal virtue is virtuality. A kind of wandering signifier, the Creature proceeds through the text triggering various signifying effects. As the reader increasingly acknowledges the larger cultural and biographical context that constitutes the penumbra of the fiction, critical representations of what the Creature represents multiply endlessly. If, for the orthodox Freudian, he is a type of the unconscious, for the Jungian he is the shadow, for the Lacanian an *objet a*, for one Romanticist a Blakean "spectre," for another a Blakean "emanation"; he also has been or can be read as Rousseau's natural man, a Wordsworthian child of nature, the isolated Romantic rebel, the misunderstood revolutionary impulse, Mary Shelley's abandoned baby self, her abandoned babe, an aberrant signifier, *différance*, or as a hypostasis of godless presumption, the monstrosity of a godless nature, analytical reasoning, or alienating labor. Like the Creature's own mythic version of himself, a freakish hybrid of Milton's Adam and Satan, all these allegorizations are exploded by the text. The alert reader, at a given moment of interpretive breakdown, will resort to another signifying chain, and thence to another, and will be left wondering whether to receive this overload of signification as a mutually enriching profusion of possibilities or as an unmeaning chaos.

While the most sensible response may be a benign ecumenical acceptance of difference, certain problems remain: for instance, how can the same text sustain divergent critical representations and what authorizes or disqualifies any representation at a particular moment? Moreover, such negative capability is likely to mask mere incapacity or a failure of will and is rarely conducive to interesting readings. Exemplary of a potentially stronger critical position are the psychoanalytic readers who would compound with the world of the text's imaginings by penetrating to its center of mystery. Entering the circle of the text and operating Freud's ingenious meaning-making machine, they will discover that an oedipal focus limits only the range of interpretive options, and if they are open to the possibility that the oedipal material they uncover may defend against other types of psychic conflict, their critical anxieties will mount. To salvage their integrity they must found a reading by arbitrarily limiting it, restricting at the same time their own cognitive, erotic, and imaginative capabilities. To construct a plausible narrative they will resort to such tactics of secondary revision as lacunae, decontextualization, distortion, and rationalized contradiction, and to persuade us that their story is not simply another revocable text they will enlist the aid of some extratextual model to underwrite both the fiction and the critical discourse. Ultimately, however, the authorizing model relies on an interpretation of how things are (or, for the growing number of the novel's psychobiographers, how things were), and whether or not the representation is privileged depends on the particular analyst's rhetorical skill and our willingness to be lied to.

A possible way out of or around this hermeneutic circle is to stop viewing the Creature as a thing apart. We might consider "meaning" as a constantly shifting relational event, asking what the Creature *No* means, at a certain point in the novel, to himself, Frankenstein, Elizabeth, or such and such a reader. The danger here is hazy relativism, an openness akin to the indifferent free trafficking that deconstructionists tend to elevate to a principle of principles. Even misreading has its map. Why one interpretive pathway should be preferred to another may be impossible to determine, but we must not forget that all must pass through the Creature, that something is there to solicit us. That something demands careful scrutiny because of its unsettling effect on our habitual ideas about what signs may be up to. Luckily barred from the overwhelming presence of the Creature, in the face of which interpretation becomes mute, we must dream our dreams of the Creature not only as a signifier in search of its proper signification but as a literal being that means only itself. The literal Creature, in other words, is as much a figuration as the figurative Creature, and in reflecting on what the letter of the text allows us to surmise about the Creature, whose "reality" we know is but a textual effect, we are always in an indeterminate borderline situation. Frankenstein never speaks more truly than when he calls the Creature his "daemon." A marginal or boundary being, the daemon is a powerful representation of our uncertain lot, suspended as we are between knowledge and power, nature and supernature, objectivity and subjectivity. Conceiving the Creature as a genius of liminality, a type of art's duplicitous interplay of revelation and concealment, restores his virtuality, which is betrayed as soon as he comes to signify something determinate. An emphasis on meaning as process also encourages the interpreter to participate in the work of the work, a dreamwork more efficacious than that of the mind abandoned to sleep. The literalizing power of Frankenstein is, of course, only a dream that haunts literature. But "labour is blossoming" (Yeats) within this marginal ontological zone, where letter and spirit forge a meaning that can never be anything more than a dreaming to signify, to become significant, to touch reality. We are touched by the passion of the signifier, a perpetually renewed *dreaming to* that no dream of satisfaction can satisfy.

Who, in our century, understood or exemplified the insistence of the dream of signification better than Freud? Psychoanalysis, for him, was always a stopgap until the real thing (biochemistry) would come along, but his inventive genius transformed the analytic field into an ample domain of spirit, an autonomous power that his system goes on calling by false names. Decentered or detraumatized, the Freudian corpus becomes an indispensable guide to the intentional play of forces that keeps meaning wandering restlessly through the mind. From Freud we can gather many enabling fictions, forms of the spirit's cunning and resourcefulness, and he can instruct us in the virtues of hovering attention, the need to look at something again and again until it begins to declare itself, and of alertness to the heterogeneous. Seeking to mediate the discrepancy between two suggestively dissimilar stories, *Frankenstein* and the orthodox psychoanalytic rendering I venture above, I now want to enter what I understand to be the true Freudian space—a place where Freud joins the company of such alienists as Blake, Milton, and Kierkegaard—as I attempt a sustained reimagining of Frankenstein's scene of creation.

II

Writing on the occasion of *Frankenstein*'s canonization, its inclusion in a "standard novels" series, Mary Shelley begins the introduction as if discharging a grim obligation to a text that should long ago have been consigned to her buried past. She is roused again, however, when she returns to the moment of the novel's origin, her waking dream of Frankenstein's emergence as a creator. Focusing on the creator's terror, she evokes the disturbing thrill of being there, in the midst of the traumatic scene, her prose mounting in intensity and shifting to the present tense as she recounts the successive stages of her vision: the powerful engine stirring to life the "hideous phantom"; Frankenstein's hysterical flight; the "horrid thing" opening the bed curtains and fixing its eyes on him, an experience of ultimate dread that shatters the vision, leaving her breathless on her "midnight pillow." What does it mean to be there, in the midst? It is to be swept up into a sublime dimension and to be faced by a dizzying void, to be at once an excited witness, the terrified artist, and the aroused form of chaos that gazes back at both creator and dreamer. Invention, Mary Shelley reflects, consists in creating "out of chaos." Once her imagination asserts itself, presenting her with the dream vision, we may associate the engine (*ingenium, genius*) with the usurping imagination, the animated Creature with the scene itself, and the chaotic mass to be set in motion with the writer's own chaos, the panic at the center of her authorial consciousness. Creator, creation, and creative agency are varying manifestations of the same anxiety that elaborates itself to compose the scene of authorship.

The novel's monstrous heart of darkness is the creation, and the creative self that inaugurates the drama resembles the "self-closd, all-repelling . . . Demon" encountered at the opening of *The Book of Urizen*. Frankenstein's founding gesture, like that of Blake's fearful demiurge, is a stepping aside, but while Urizen secedes from Eternity, Frankenstein absents himself from our world of ordinary awareness and relatedness, which recedes from him in much the manner that a dream fades at the instant of awakening. Severing all contact with his family, other beings, and familiar nature, he is intent on hollowing out a zone in reality where he can be utterly alone. This ingressive movement is attended by self-loss, a radical shrinkage of his empirical self, and self-aggrandizement, a heightening of his isolate selfhood to daemonic status. He becomes a force instead of a person as all the energy of his being concentrates on his grand project: "My mind was filled with one thought, one conception, one purpose"; "a resistless, and almost frantic, impulse urged me forward; I seemed to have lost all soul or sensation but for this one pursuit." The animation project, like the object intended by the Freudian libido, is a secondary affair. What matters is that it enkindles in the projector a lust for self-presence so intense that it drives out of consciousness everything except itself.

Reality must yield if the self is to appear, and Frankenstein's primary creative act is to originate his own creative self.

The vertiginous upward fall that founds the creative self coincides with a rupture between daemonic mind and all that is not mind. What may loosely be termed consciousness (of self, an extravagantly augmented self so full of itself as to allow neither time nor space for self-awareness) and unconsciousness (of the normative world from which the self has detached itself) are twin-born, factoring out as discrete loci that mark the decisiveness of Frankenstein's psychic dislocation. Only in the catastrophic nature of this birth is there any significant point of contact with the repressive process that institutes ego and id as opposing agencies in the Freudian economy. Narcissism and, probably closer, psychosis are the appropriate psychoanalytic analogues, though the usefulness of these nosological entities here is questionable. I see no need, for example, to posit a specific libidinal stage or fixation point to which Frankenstein is regressing. But everything would resolve itself into a structural conflict anyway: Frankenstein's oedipal trouble impels his defensive "episode," which signals a victory of the forces of repression; and with the creation he spills back into the domain of assured analytic knowledge, the Creature amounting to a bizarre symptomatic return of the repressed that can be interpreted in the same way as the dream of a neurotic. For the psychoanalyst, then, the Creature is a figure that redoubles Frankenstein's literal unconscious complex, which is already present as an a priori with a determinate constitution; in fact, however, he is an autonomous agent, not a psychic agency, and Frankenstein's supposed unconscious is a figurative device, a critic's overhasty recourse designed to mediate or neutralize a puzzling discontinuity.

By what name shall we invoke discontinuity? For Milton in *Paradise Lost* it is Hell, a space carved out in the universe to receive the daemonic selfhood of Satan, for whom everything is a universe of death. The depth of one's particular hell is an index of how far one has fallen away from what might be perceived or known. The unconscious, in other words, is a modality of subjective experience whose meaning is estrangement. What Frankenstein creates, in order to create, is distance between his daemonized self and a newly alienated reality, and it scarcely matters whether we conceive this space as interior or exterior since it is a fantastic medial zone where the boundaries between self and world are impossible to distinguish. Within this void, between two created "nothings," self-consciousness appears. It is the place into which the baffled residue of Frankenstein's ordinary self has been cast. From its vantage, somewhere in the corner of Frankenstein's mind, it takes notes, watching with horrified fascination the extravagant career of a stranger that is also an uncanny variation of the self.

Out of this phantom place, in addition, the Creature emerges, as Blake's Enitharmon emanates from Los once Los "closes" with the death image of Urizen, thus embracing the world view of the solipsistically withdrawn creating mind. The ungraspable Enitharmon, Los's loss and shadowed gain, embodies the suddenly exterior, objectified space that has opened up between Los and Eternity, or Los's alienated potential. The Creature is similarly a token of loss, a complex representation of the estranged universe Frankenstein has summoned into being by pushing away reality. Yet does the Creature, strictly speaking, represent Frankenstein's alienated potential? I suppose he can be read as the responsive, sympathic imagination Frankenstein suppresses in order to create. From the psychoanalytic perspective, such repression would be very odd: imagine the id repressing the sublimated ego. The repression hypothesis must be rejected in any event because the Creature is something radically new and different, no more a double or a part of Frankenstein than Enitharmon is of Los. Instead, these emanative beings "stand for" their creators in the sense that they are interpolations, "transitional objects" (Winnicott) or texts, intended to rectify a catastrophic disalignment of self and world.

The creation is at once a new departure for Frankenstein and the climax of a developmental process that, as Wordsworth says, "hath no beginning." Frankenstein's narrative begins with an idyll of domestic bliss: in the protected enclave of his household all are incomparably virtuous and lovable; affections go deep, and yet everyone lives on the surface. Of course, it is all a lie, but the reader should be troubled by this absurdity no more than by the newborn Creature's walking off with Frankenstein's coat as protection against the cold. Just as anyone who wishes can discover the source of an individual's troubles in the past, since so much happened "there," readers inclined to locate the cause of Frankenstein's aberration in his youth will see what they expect to see in his narrative or will find that what they seek is all the more confirmed by its absence from the account. His fall may have been occasioned by Elizabeth's admission into the family circle, by William's birth, by the sinister "silken cord" of parental constriction, or by a repressed primal-scene trauma. It doesn't matter: any psychotrauma is as true or as false as any other. Like all of us, Frankenstein begins fallen—or, better, falling. The brief idyll of his youth gives him something to fall away from; and the more remotely idealized the starting point, the more absolute or self-defining is his point of departure. Frankenstein simply announces that, as far back as he can remember, "the world was to me a secret which I desired to divine." That is, the fall from the wholeness of origins is rooted in his lust to overtake a hidden, receding presence, or a tantalizing absence, that lies behind appearances and disturbs his contact with things. This dualizing consciousness is a given of his temperament, the destiny-assigned identity theme that he lives out in the sphere of science but that he could have expressed as well in exploration or authorship. Can we improve on Frankenstein's version, or on Coleridge's characterization of Iago as "a motiveless malignity"? The aptly named Iago is the ego principle, the sublimely arbitrary human will that originates everything, including all myths of a catastrophic or transcendental point of spiritual origination, and motive hunting no more explains his willfulness than it does Desdemona's love for Othello.

Motivation, like sequential logic, is a falsification the mind cannot do without. The signal importance Frankenstein ascribes to the death of his mother suggests that the reanimation project is a deferred reaction to this event, which he terms "the first misfortune of my life . . . an omen . . . of my future misery." He dwells on the "irreparable evil" brought about by the rending of ties and on the "void" created by death, which he raises to quasi-supernatural status as "the spoiler." Presumably her death reactivates an original anxiety of deprivation associated with the departure of the maternal body, and the irrevocable loss of the mother, the primary focus of the child's reality bondings, could help to explain the intensification of Frankenstein's temperamental dualism. But while psychoanalytic theory is suggestive here, it is too restrictively bound to a particular mythic version of the past, too fetishistically centered on one of many possible mythic representations of loss. Like the oak-shattering bolt, the death of the mother is preeminently a narcissistic insult for Frankenstein. Confronted by the fact of death, he is overtaken by a primordial anxiety, not an anxiety-provoking repressed wish; and although such anxiety is apt to recoil from any number of fancied antagonists, its proper object is the most inclusive and irreducible of forces: life, our human life, in relation to which death is not an external agency but an internal component. Yet, as Kierkegaard knew, consciousness of this radical fault in existence need not, or need not only, paralyze the spirit. Dread, and perhaps even the fear of being delivered over to it, can be a sublime energizer, arousing the infinite spirit that longs for a house as large as itself.

Seeking to undo the consequences of sexuality, the sin of being born of woman, Frankenstein engages in a pursuit at once regressive and projective, mobilizing old energies in an attempt to discover a new meaning for himself. Adrift for a time after his mother's death, he is eager, once he leaves for the university, to cast off his dependence and put his talents to work. All that remains is for Waldman's sermon, perhaps more the sheer power of his voice than his overt message, to render an occasion for Frankenstein's restless drive for autonomy:

> Such were the professor's words—rather let me say such the words of fate. . . . As he went on, I felt as if my soul were grappling with a palpable enemy; one by one the various keys were touched which formed the mechanism of my being. . . . So much has been done, exclaimed the soul of Frankenstein—more, far more, will I achieve . . . I will pioneer a new way, explore unknown powers, and unfold to the world the deepest mysteries of creation.

This powerfully charged moment of conversion, or reconversion, founds Frankenstein as an artist. From the struggle of his second birth he emerges as a force of destiny, genius in a human form, first pronouncing the fateful name of the modern Prometheus: *franken Stein*, the free rock, the free-unfree man.

After two years of reviewing the current state of scientific knowledge, Frankenstein is abruptly halted by an audacious, yet for him inevitable, question: "Whence . . . did the principle of life proceed?" The way is opened for his first descent into the world of the tomb: "I beheld the corruption of death succeed to the blooming cheek of life; I saw how the worm inherited the wonders of the eye and brain." At this stage Frankenstein presents himself as a detached observer of death's work, and nature offers little resistance to his inquiries. "A sudden light" breaks "from the midst of this darkness," whereupon he is dazzled to discover himself the first of mortals capable of disentangling life from death. Modern criticism, generally empowered by demystifying reversals, has tended both to devalue Frankenstein's discovery, regarding his life principle as a type of natural energy rather than as a genuine first, and to view his enthusiasm as a mechanical operation of the spirit. Although the great Romantic faith in the omnipotence of thought is unquestionably allied to the scientist's baleful drive for manipulative control, they remain very distinct forms of the Cartesian legacy. To the extent that the artist in Frankenstein collapses into the technician he is a loser. But now, as he stands at the source, Frankenstein is a sublime quester who has found his muse, an answering subject to inspire and direct the quest, and his delight is that of a man who has come to recognize the glory of his own inner source, his originative *I am*.

Once Frankenstein begins to describe the lengthy creation process his hitherto sequential narrative becomes curiously perturbed. The style is spasmodic, juxtapositive, and repetitive, obscuring temporal relations yet underscoring how radically divided the creator is. We hear from a practical Frankenstein, who reasons that even an imperfect effort will lay the ground for future successes; a secretly selfish utopian idealist, who dreams of a new species blessing him "as its creator and source"; and a domestic Frankenstein, who procrastinates "all that related to my feelings of affection until the great object, which swallowed up every habit of my nature, should be completed." Being swallowed up is the principal terror of the narrative consciousness dominating these pages, a depersonalized, though suffering, observer of the wreck Frankenstein is becoming. Little is heard from the daemonized Frankenstein, in part because his experience of sublime uplift is wordless and in part because this "hurricane" has no time for words, though for the troubled eye of the storm time is agonizingly slow. Complicating matters is the superimposition of the narrative present on an episode that the fallen Frankenstein can be relied on to misconstrue, so that the complex web of the account becomes virtually impossible to unweave. Then, we may surmise, a dialectic of the following sort was at work: driving out and driven in, the creative self is agonistic, aggressively excluding otherness, and hence agonized, defensively immuring itself in resistance to any foreign body that would encroach on its sublime solitude; the barrier keeps breaking, however, leading to disabling bouts of self-consciousness, which in turn provoke even more audacious sublime rushes that threaten to overwhelm the ordinary self, that residual underconsciousness which clings ever more desperately to its bewildered identity. How one interprets the meaning of the entire experience—whether from the point of view of the daemonic self or from that of the ordinary self—probably tells more about the interpreter than about the experience itself, just as the Abyssinian maid of "Kubla Khan" emerges as the muse of paradise or the voice of the abyss depending on whether one stands inside or outside the magic circle of the conclusion.

The breathlessly eager self that is in, or is, the enthusiasm soars above the body that is taking shape. Frankenstein's workshop is located "in a solitary chamber, or rather cell, at the top of the house, and separated from all the other apartments." This is a masterful emblem of the mind that is its own place. The windows are barred, at least for the enthusiast, whose eyes remain "insensible to the charms of nature." Those "charms" are an interpolation of Frankenstein the notetaker or narrator; the creator is an innerness—pure, unconditioned spirit—seeking innerness—the life or light in, but not of, things. Things themselves do not exist for him except as "lifeless matter" to be animated, the *fort* to his *da* (*sein*), and the more they are leveled to a deadening continuity the more discontinuous is the fiery spirit that would stamp its image on a world rendered pliable to its projects and projections.

The problem is that if the sublime artist is to "pour a torrent of light into our dark world" of mortal life, he must take a detour through reality. To wrest the spirit from things he must, for a second time, penetrate into the center of the earth, and to prepare a frame for the reception of life he must now not only see and know but also touch the body of death. Undertaking a shamanistic descent into chaos, a place of "filthy creation" where life and death conspire to breed monstrous shapes, Frankenstein is flooded with nausea: "Who shall conceive the horrors of my secret toil, as I dabbled among the unhallowed damps of the grave, or tortured the living animal to animate the lifeless clay?" Is Frankenstein speaking of vivisection, or is the tortured living body his own? His aggression, whether directed outward or against himself, recalls that of Blake's Urizen:

> Times on times he divided, & measur'd
> Space by space in his ninefold darkness
> Unseen, unknown! changes appeard
> In his desolate mountains rifted furious
> By the black winds of perturbation
>
> For he strove in battles dire
> In unseen conflictions with shapes
> Bred from his forsaken wilderness
> (*The Book of Urizen* 1.2–3)

Frankenstein too is entrapped by his own phantasmagoria. The oppressively close, enveloping tomb world into which he descends is a self-engendered abyss that discloses what our finite bodily ground looks like from the heights to which the spirit has ascended. Transforming an evacuated reality into a grotesque naturalization and the denied natural passions into a perversely eroticized shadow life, the sublime artist's exaggerated distance from things has also transformed him into a graveyard poet. In short, Frankenstein has discovered, or invented, an inchoate version of the Freudian unconscious.

Frankenstein's aggression and perverse perception are inscribed in the Creature's appearance. The artist envisioned something quite different: "How can I . . . delineate that wretch whom with such infinite pains and care I had endeavoured to form? His limbs were in proportion, and I had selected his features as beautiful." What *did* Frankenstein intend? Treading "heaven in my thoughts . . . exulting in my powers," he conceived the Creature as a representation of the transfigured creative self, a grandiose embodiment of the creator's mind. But it is also a desperate compromise, designed to mend an intolerable dualism. The beautiful Creature of Frankenstein's imaginings is analogous to Sin, the perfect narcissistic image of Satan, the interior paramour who explodes from his brain when heaven rolls away from him and with whom he proceeds to copulate; Frankenstein's dread monster corresponds to Sin's unrecognized "nether shape," but even more closely to Death, that chaotic "darkness visible," who is the ultimate issue of Satan's deranged spirit, his love of his own thought. The moving Creature, like Death, is unrepresentable. However, directly after the infusion of life, while the Creature is still dazed, Frankenstein ventures the novel's only description of this formless form:

> Beautiful!—Great God! His yellow skin scarcely covered the work of muscles and arteries beneath; his hair was of a lustrous black, and flowing; his teeth of a pearly whiteness; but these luxuriances only formed a more horrid contrast with the watery eyes, that seemed almost of the same colour as the dun white sockets in which they were set, his shrivelled complexion and straight black lips.

An "unearthly" figure, the Creature bodies forth the horrid contrast between heaven and hell that Frankenstein experiences as a dizzying, instantaneous descent.

How is one to explain this catastrophic turn? The only way to fathom the Creature's appearance, which is more a rhetorical effect than a natural fact, is to comprehend how it was made. For Frankenstein, putting together and dismembering are one. The parts he chooses are beautiful, but they are monstrous in conjunction—or, rather, since the Creature lacks a phenomenological center, in their absolute disjunction. Frankenstein is similarly unbalanced, a confused collectivity. The daemonized self that initiates the project is a force inimical to form, and it cannot see or guide properly from the heights. The normative self, desperately in need of bridging back to reality, patches over the rift in the fabric of Frankenstein's existence as best it can. But although its eyeballs start "from their sockets in attending to the details," it cannot recollect the original inspiration. The result of all this frantic alienated labor is a being geared to self-torment. As such, the Creature is also a figure that reveals, with more startling accuracy and profundity than discursive reason can command, the existential condition of its progenitor: his relation-disrelation to his world, his thoughts, and himself. The incomplete Creature, unmated and unmatable, an inconceivably lonely free-standing unit whose inside is hopelessly divided from its outside, is indeed a "filthy type" of the modern Prometheus.

Any representation of the creative process, whether the novel's narrative or my analytic account, is bound to distort the experience of the whole self. Suspended between heaven and hell, those absolutely disjoined fictive polarities that are in fact mutually sustaining correlates, the creator is at once ravished and ravaged by sublimity. He is filled and swallowed up, but not entirely full or emptied out; for to be wholly abandoned to the sublime would amount to autism, and there would no longer be a self to experience the uplift or downfall. It is always, to modify Emerson slightly, a case of I *and* the abyss. Since he cannot be the thing itself and cannot be nothing, Frankenstein is a spirit destined to "exult in the agony of the torturing flames." Another name for this giant agony is despair. "Despair," writes Kierkegaard, cannot

> consume the eternal thing, the self, which is the ground of despair, whose worm dieth not, and whose fire is not quenched. Yet despair is precisely *self*-consuming, but it is an impotent self-consumption. . . . This is the hot incitement, or the cold fire in despair, the gnawing canker whose movement is constantly inward, deeper and deeper. . . .

This precisely is the reason why he despairs . . . because he cannot consume himself, cannot get rid of himself, cannot become nothing. This is the potentiated formula for despair, the rising of the fever in the sickness of the self.

(*The Sickness unto Death*)

Kierkegaard, dangerously on the verge of becoming the dread itself, is a better guide here than Freud, the great analyst of the concept of dread. As Kierkegaard would have it, Frankenstein is a prisoner of despair because his volatile spirit desires only to augment itself, because the self is not "grounded transparently in the Power which posited it." That power, which may simply be a potentiated form of the despairing spirit, exists beyond the purview of Mary Shelley's fiction. But *Frankenstein* is empowered, and at times disabled, by a despair over the human condition, whose limits condemn the creator's sublime quest to the status of an extravagant, desperate wish. The novel's wisdom, not only imperfectly expressed by an advocacy of domestic bliss but in fact undercut by overt moralizing, is that we need "keeping," that we must be concrete in the same measure as we are abstract and that we must abide with the antinomies (life and death, ideality and actuality, will and fate) that constitute our ground. Frankenstein may be said to err in misreading both his own reality and the larger reality that circumscribes his existence. No matter how great the spirit within him, the universal life principle he thinks he has captured, although it is not merely a trick of spirit, can never become his instrument for correcting existence. It "was now within my grasp," he says; he adds, however, that "the information I had obtained was of a nature rather to direct my endeavours so soon as I should point them towards the object of my search. . . . I was like the Arabian who had been buried with the dead, and found a passage to life, aided only by one glimmering, and seemingly ineffectual, light." Dazzled by an obscure revelation, he can only move toward the light, for the power sources he taps is a constituent element in an ongoing process, a continuum of animation and deanimation according to whose subtle rhythm of recurrence we live and die every moment. Frankenstein is a thief of fire, and the utmost he can do is to transmit the power to a body capable of sustaining life.

His nervous symptoms become increasingly pathological as the time for the Creature's inspiration nears, and once he is about to perform the deed, finding himself in a recognizably realistic setting,

Frankenstein is less anxious than melancholic, as though calamity has already struck. What possible act or object could satisfy the aspirations of the uncreated soul? The dream of the sublime artist's overflowing fullness is grotesquely parodied as Frankenstein sickens into creation: "the rain pattered dismally against the panes, and my candle was nearly burnt out, when, by the glimmer of the half-extinguished light, I saw the dull yellow eye of the creature open." What is bracketed here, at the decisive moment of Frankenstein's reentry into reality, is the infusion of the spark of life. The creative act is a mindless reflex, an indication that the creator has fallen away from his desire into a void that nothing can fill but that somehow must be limited, as in *The Book of Urizen*, by a barrier of "solid obstruction." The Creature, though not quite setting a limit to Frankenstein's nightmare, is hell's bottom. Landing there, Frankenstein sees his Creature for the first time when its eyes open, a negative epiphany revealing to him that he is not alone, that he too is now visible. The nightmare follows, with its horrific climactic emblem of the condition of corporeality, and he wakens to confront the self-impelled Creature, the living image of death this new Orpheus has brought back from the house of the dead. The creator's terror attests to his lack of mastery, the grim fact of his own creatureliness, which is what set the creative process in motion. Beholding the Creature, Frankenstein is back at his original impasse, uncannily subject to the recurrence of his dread of time, space, and the body of death.

It is impossible to know what Frankenstein apprehends at the pivotal instant when his half-extinguished candle is eclipsed by the Creature's dull yellow eye, but the former seeker of the inner light almost immediately fixates on appearances. The overwhelming irony is that Frankenstein has opened up a space in reality for the emergence of something radically new, realizing the power to make literally present that the poets have always dreamed of. A presence so full that it is as unapproachable as light or an absence so great that it confounds the representational faculties, the Creature is the sublime or grotesque thing itself. Frankenstein's all too human failure of response is to petrify his living artifact into an otherness that cannot be restituted by mind. The Creature becomes a blocking agent, standing between Frankenstein and the normative world he longs to rejoin, and an uncanny reminder of the creator's alienated majesty, the sublime experience from which he is henceforth irremediably estranged. This unproductive misreading, though saving him from an encounter with

Dread itself, condemns both Creature and creator to anguished incompleteness. Locked into an interminable pursuit of the shadow he has become, Frankenstein emerges as the man who cannot emerge, a prisoner of the passage arrested at the moment of his falling away from his own possible sublimity. The final irony is that his solitude is confirmed. Frankenstein achieves his own separate consciousness of himself as the most wretched of mortals. But even if his egotism is such that he glories in this doom as the token of a special destiny, he has become just another Gothic hero-villain, a tiresome neurotic whose presence impoverishes the larger portion of the novel that bears his name.

My Monster / My Self

Barbara Johnson

To judge from recent trends in scholarly as well as popular literature, three crucial questions can be seen to stand at the forefront of today's preoccupations: the question of mothering, the question of the woman writer, and the question of autobiography. Although these questions and current discussions of them often appear unrelated to each other, it is my intention here to explore some ways in which the three questions *are* profoundly interrelated, and to attempt to shed new light on each by approaching it via the others. I shall base my remarks upon two twentieth-century theoretical studies—Nancy Friday's *My Mother/My Self* and Dorothy Dinnerstein's *The Mermaid and the Minotaur*—and one nineteenth-century Gothic novel, *Frankenstein; or, The Modern Prometheus,* written by Mary Shelley, whose importance for literary history has until quite recently been considered to arise not from her own writings but from the fact that she was the second wife of poet Percy Bysshe Shelley and the daughter of political philosopher William Godwin and pioneering feminist Mary Wollstonecraft.

All three of these books, in strikingly diverse ways, offer a critique of the institution of parenthood. *The Mermaid and the Minotaur* is an analysis of the damaging effects of the fact that human infants are cared for almost exclusively by women. "What the book's title as a whole is meant to connote," writes Dinnerstein, "is both (a) our longstanding general awareness of our uneasy, ambiguous position in the animal kingdom, and (b) a more specific awareness: that until we

From *Diacritics* 12, no. 2 (Summer 1982). © 1982 by the Johns Hopkins University Press.

grow strong enough to renounce the pernicious forms of collaboration between the sexes, both man and woman will remain semi-human, monstrous." Even as Dinnerstein describes convincingly the types of imbalance and injustice the prevailing asymmetry in gender relations produces, she also analyzes the reasons for our refusal to abandon the very modes of monstrousness from which we suffer most. Nancy Friday's book, which is subtitled "A Daughter's Search for Identity," argues that the mother's repression of herself necessitated by the myth of maternal love creates a heritage of self-rejection, anger, and duplicity that makes it difficult for the daughter to seek any emotional satisfaction other than the state of idealized symbiosis that both mother and daughter continue to punish themselves for never having been able to achieve. Mary Shelley's *Frankenstein* is an even more elaborate and unsettling formulation of the relation between parenthood and monstrousness. It is the story of two antithetical modes of parenting that give rise to two increasingly parallel lives—the life of Victor Frankenstein, who is the beloved child of two doting parents, and the life of the monster he single-handedly creates, who is immediately spurned and abandoned by his creator. The fact that in the end both characters reach an equal degree of alienation and self-torture and indeed become indistinguishable as they pursue each other across the frozen polar wastes indicates that the novel is, among other things, a study of the impossibility of finding an adequate model for what a parent should be.

All three books agree, then, that in the existing state of things there is something inherently monstrous about the prevailing parental arrangements. While Friday and Dinnerstein, whose analyses directly address the problem of sexual difference, suggest that this monstrousness is curable, Mary Shelley, who does not explicitly locate the self's monstrousness in its gender arrangements, appears to dramatize divisions within the human being that are so much a part of being human that no escape from monstrousness seems possible.

What I will try to do here is to read these three books not as mere *studies* of the monstrousness of selfhood, not as mere *accounts* of human monsterdom in general, but precisely as autobiographies in their own right, as textual dramatizations of the very problems with which they deal. None of the three books, of course, presents itself explicitly as autobiography. Yet each includes clear moments of employment of the autobiographical—not the purely authorial—first-person pronoun. In each case the autobiographical reflex is triggered by the resistance and ambivalence involved in the very writing of the book. What I shall argue here is that what is specifically feminist in each book is directly related to this struggle for feminine authorship.

The notion that *Frankenstein* can somehow be read as the autobiography of a woman would certainly appear at first sight to be ludicrous. The novel, indeed, presents not one but *three* autobiographies of men. Robert Walton, an Arctic explorer on his way to the North Pole, writes home to his sister of his encounter with Victor Frankenstein, who tells Walton the story of his painstaking creation and unexplained abandonment of a nameless monster who suffers excruciating and fiendish loneliness, and who tells Frankenstein *his* life story in the middle pages of the book. The three male autobiographies motivate themselves as follows:

> *Walton (to his sister):* "You will rejoice to hear that no disaster has accompanied the commencement of an enterprise which you have regarded with such evil forebodings. I arrived here yesterday, and my first task is to assure my dear sister of my welfare."

> *Frankenstein (with his hands covering his face, to Walton, who has been speaking of his scientific ambition):* "Unhappy man! Do you share my madness? Have you drunk also of the intoxicating draught? Hear me; let me reveal my tale, and you will dash the cup from your lips!"

> *Monster (to Frankenstein):* "I entreat you to hear me before you give vent to your hatred on my devoted head." [Frankenstein:] "Begone! I will not hear you. There can be no community between you and me [. . .]" [Monster places his hands before Frankenstein's eyes:] "Thus I take from thee a sight which you abhor. Still thou canst listen to me and grant me thy compassion . . . God, in pity, made man beautiful and alluring, after his own image; but my form is a filthy type of yours, more horrid even from the very resemblance."

All three autobiographies here are clearly attempts at persuasion rather than simple accounts of facts. They all depend on a presupposition of *resemblance* between teller and addressee: Walton assures his sister that he has not really left the path she would wish for him, that he still resembles *her*. Frankenstein recognizes in Walton an image of himself and rejects in the monster a resemblance he does not wish to acknowledge. The teller is in each case speaking into a mirror of his own transgression. The tale is designed to reinforce the resemblance between teller and listener so that somehow transgression can be eliminated. Yet the desire for resemblance, the desire to create a being like oneself—which is the autobiographical desire par excellence—is also the *central* transgression in Mary Shelley's novel. What is at stake in Frankenstein's workshop of filthy creation is precisely the possibility of shaping a life in one's own image: Frankenstein's monster can thus be seen as a figure for autobiography as such. Victor Frankenstein, then, has twice obeyed the impulse to construct an image of himself: on the first occasion he creates a monster, and on the second he tries to explain to Walton the causes and consequences of the first. *Frankenstein* can be read as the story of autobiography as the attempt to neutralize the monstrosity of autobiography. Simultaneously a revelation and a coverup, autobiography would appear to constitute itself as in some way a repression of autobiography.

These three fictive male autobiographies are embedded within a thin introductory frame, added in 1831, in which Mary Shelley herself makes the repression of her own autobiographical impulse explicit:

> The publishers of the standard novels, in selecting *Frankenstein* for one of their series, expressed a wish that I should furnish them with some account of the origin of the story. [. . .] It is true that I am very averse to bringing myself forward in print, but as my account will only appear as an appendage to a former production, and as it will be confined to such topics as have connection with my authorship alone, I can scarcely accuse myself of a personal intrusion.

Mary Shelley, here, rather than speaking *into* a mirror, is speaking as an appendage to a text. It might perhaps be instructive to ask whether this change of status has anything to do with the problem of specifically *feminine* autobiography. In a humanistic tradition in which *man* is the measure of all things, how does an appendage go about telling the story of her life?

Before pursuing this question further, I would like to turn to a more explicit version of surreptitious feminine autobiography. Of the three books under discussion, Nancy Friday's account of the mother/daughter relationship relies the most heavily on the facts of the author's life in order to demonstrate its thesis. Since the author grew up without a father, she shares with Frankenstein's monster some of the problems of coming from a single-parent household. The book begins with a chapter entitled "Mother Love," of which the first two sentences are: "I have always lied to my mother. And she to me." Interestingly, the book carries the following dedication: "When I stopped seeing my mother with the eyes of a child, I saw the woman who helped me give birth to myself. This book is for Jane Colbert Friday Scott." How, then, can we be sure that this huge book is not itself another lie to the mother it is dedicated to? Is autobiography somehow always in the process of symbolically killing the mother off by telling her the lie that we have given birth to ourselves? On page 460, Nancy Friday is still not sure what kind of lie she has told. She writes: "I am suddenly afraid that the mother I have depicted throughout this book is false." Whose life is this, anyway? This question cannot be resolved by a book that sees the "daughter's search for identity" as the necessity of choosing *between* symbiosis and separation, *between* the mother and the autonomous self. As long as this polarity remains unquestioned, the autobiography of Nancy Friday becomes the drawing and redrawing of the portrait of Jane Colbert Friday Scott. The most truly autobiographical moments occur not in expressions of triumphant separation but in descriptions of the way the book itself attempts to resist its own writing. At the end of the chapter on loss of virginity, Nancy Friday writes:

> It took me twenty-one years to give up my virginity. In some similar manner I am unable to let go of this chapter. . . .
>
> It is no accident that wrestling with ideas of loss of virginity immediately bring me to a dream of losing my mother. This chapter has revealed a split in me. Intellectually, I think of myself as a sexual person, just as I had intellectually been able to put my ideas for this chapter down on paper. Subjectively, I don't want to face what I have written: that the declaration of full sexual independence is the declaration of separation from my mother. As long as I don't finish this chapter, as long as I don't let myself understand the implications of what I've written, I can maintain the illusion, at least, that I can be sexual and have my mother's love and approval too.

As long as sexual identity and mother's judgment are linked as antithetical and exclusive poles of the daughter's problem, the "split" she describes will prevent her from ever completing her declaration of sexual independence. "Full sexual independence" is shown by the book's own resistance to be as illusory and as mystifying an ideal as the notion of "mother love" that Friday so lucidly rejects.

Dinnerstein's autobiographical remarks are more muted, although her way of letting the reader know that the book was written partly in mourning for her husband subtly underlies its persuasive seriousness. In her gesture of rejecting more traditional forms of scholarship, she pleads not for the validity but for the urgency of her message:

> Right now, what I think is that the kind of work of which this is an example is centrally necessary work. Whether our understanding makes a difference or not, we must try to understand what is threatening to kill us off as fully and clearly as we can. . . . What [this book] is, then, is not a scholarly book: it makes no effort to survey the relevant literature. Not only would that task be (for me) unmanageably huge. It would also be against my principles. I *believe* in reading unsystematically and taking notes erratically. Any effort to form a rational policy about what to take in, out of the inhuman flood of printed human utterance that pours over us daily, feels to me like a self-deluded exercise in pseudomastery.

The typographical form of this book bears out this belief in renouncing the appearance of mastery: there are two kinds of footnotes, some at the foot of the page and some at the back of the book; there are sections between chapters with unaligned right-hand margins which are called "Notes toward the next chapter." And there are bold-face inserts which dialogue with the controversial points in the main exposition. Clearly, great pains have been taken to let as many seams as possible show in the fabric of the argument. The preface goes on:

> I mention these limitations in a spirit not of apology but of warning. To the extent that it succeeds in communicating its point at all, this book will necessarily enrage the reader. What it says is emotionally threatening. (*Part of why it has taken me so long to finish it is that I am threatened by it myself*)
> [emphasis mine].

My book is roughly sutured, says Dinnerstein, and it is threatening. This description sounds uncannily like a description of Victor Frankenstein's monster. Indeed, Dinnerstein goes on to warn the reader not to be tempted to avoid the threatening message by pointing to superficial flaws in its physical make-up. The reader of *Frankenstein*, too, would be well advised to look beyond the monster's physical deformity, both for his fearsome power and for his beauty. There are indeed numerous ways in which *The Mermaid and the Minotaur* can be seen as a modern rewriting of *Frankenstein*.

Dinnerstein's book situates its plea for two-sex parenting firmly in an apparently twentieth-century double bind: the realization that the very technological advances that make it possible to change the structure of parenthood also threaten to extinguish earthly life altogether. But it is startling to note that this seemingly contemporary pairing of the question of parenthood with a love-hate relation to technology is already at work in Mary Shelley's novel, where the spectacular scientific discovery of the secrets of animation produces a terrifyingly vengeful creature who attributes his evil impulses to his inability to find or to become a parent. Subtitled "The Modern Prometheus," *Frankenstein* itself indeed refers back to a myth that already links scientific ambivalence with the origin of mankind. Prometheus, the fire bringer, the giver of both creation and destruction, is also said by some accounts to be the father of the human race. Ambivalence toward technology can thus be seen as a displaced version of the love-hate relation we have toward our own children.

It is only recently that critics have begun to see Victor Frankenstein's disgust at the sight of his creation as a study of postpartum depression, as a representation of maternal rejection of a newborn infant, and to relate the entire novel to Mary Shelley's mixed feelings about motherhood. Having lived through an unwanted pregnancy from a man married to someone else only to see that baby die, followed by a second baby named William—which is the name of the Monster's first murder victim—Mary Shelley, at the age of only eighteen, must have had excruciatingly divided emotions. Her own mother, indeed, had died upon giving her birth. The idea that a mother can loathe, fear, and reject her baby has until recently been one of the most repressed of psychoanalytical insights, although it is of course already implicit in the story of Oedipus, whose parents cast him out as an infant to die. What is threatening about each of these books is the way in which its critique of the *role* of the mother touches on primitive terrors of the mother's rejection of the child. Each of these women writers *does* in her way reject the child as part of her coming to grips with the untenable nature of mother love: Nancy Friday decides not to have children, Dorothy Dinnerstein argues that men as well as women should do the mothering, and Mary Shelley describes a parent who flees in disgust from the repulsive being to whom he has just given birth.

Yet it is not merely in its depiction of the ambivalence of motherhood that Mary Shelley's novel can be read as autobiographical. In the introductory note added in 1831, she writes:

> The publishers of the standard novels, in selecting *Frankenstein* for one of their series, expressed a wish that I should furnish them with some account of the origin of the story. I am the more willing to comply because I shall thus give a general answer to the question so very frequently asked me—how I, then a young girl, came to think of and to *dilate upon* so very hideous an idea [emphasis mine].

As this passage makes clear, readers of Mary Shelley's novel had frequently expressed the feeling that a young girl's fascination with the idea of monstrousness was somehow monstrous in itself. When Mary ends her introduction to the re-edition of her novel with the words: "And now, once again, I bid my hideous progeny go forth and prosper," the reader begins to suspect that there may perhaps be meaningful parallels between Victor's creation of his monster and Mary's creation of her book.

Such parallels are indeed unexpectedly pervasive. The impulse to write the book and the desire to search for the secrets of animation both arise under the same seemingly trivial circumstances: the necessity of finding something to read on a rainy day. During inclement weather on a family vacation, Victor Frankenstein happens upon the writings of Cornelius Agrippa, and is immediately fired with the longing to penetrate the secrets of life and death. Similarly, it was during a wet, ungenial summer in Switzerland that Mary, Shelley, Byron, and several others picked up a volume of ghost stories and decided to write a collection of spine-tingling tales of their own. Moreover, Mary's discovery of the subject she would write about is described in almost exactly the same words as Frankenstein's discovery of the principle of life: "Swift as light and as cheering was the idea that broke in upon me," writes Mary in her introduction, while Frankenstein says: "From the midst of this darkness a sudden light broke in upon me." In both cases the sudden flash of inspiration must be supported by the meticulous gathering of heterogeneous, ready-made materials: Frankenstein collects bones and organs; Mary records overheard discussions of scientific questions that lead her to her sudden vision of monstrous creation. "Invention," she writes of the process of writing, but her words apply equally well to Frankenstein's labors, "Invention . . . does not consist in creating out of the void, but out of chaos; the materials must, in the first place, be afforded: it can give form to dark, shapeless substances but cannot bring into being the substance itself." Perhaps the most revealing indication of Mary's identification of Frankenstein's activity with her own is to be found in her use of the word "artist" on two different occasions to qualify the "pale student of unhallowed arts": "His success would terrify the *artist*," she writes of the catastrophic moment of creation, while Frankenstein confesses to Walton: "I appeared rather like one doomed by slavery to toil in the mines, or any other unwholesome trade than an *artist* occupied by his favorite employment."

Frankenstein, in other words, can be read as the story of the experience of writing *Frankenstein*. What is at stake in Mary's introduction as well as in the novel is the description of a *primal scene of creation*. *Frankenstein* combines a monstrous answer to two of the most fundamental questions one can ask: where do babies come from? and where do stories come from? In both cases, the scene of creation is described, but the answer to these questions is still withheld.

But what can Victor Frankenstein's workshop of filthy creation teach us about the specificity of *female* authorship? At first sight, it would seem that *Frankenstein* is much more striking for its avoidance of the question of femininity than for its insight into it. All the interesting, complex characters in the book are male, and their deepest attachments are to other males. The females, on the other hand, are beautiful, gentle, selfless, boring nurturers and victims who never experience inner conflict or true desire. Monstrousness is so incompatible with femininity that Frankenstein cannot even complete the female companion that his creature so eagerly awaits.

On the other hand, the story of Frankenstein is, after all, the story of a man who usurps the female role by physically giving birth to a child. It would be tempting, therefore, to conclude that Mary Shelley, surrounded as she then was by the male poets Byron and Shelley, and mortified for days by her inability to think of a story to contribute to their ghost-story contest, should have fictively transposed her own frustrated female pen envy into a tale of catastrophic male womb envy.

In this perspective, Mary's book would suggest that a woman's desire to write and a man's desire to give birth would both be capable only of producing monsters.

Yet clearly things cannot be so simple. As the daughter of a famous feminist whose *Vindication of the Rights of Woman* she was in the process of rereading during the time she was writing *Frankenstein*, Mary Shelley would have no reason to believe that writing was not proper for a woman. Indeed, as she says in her introduction, Mary was practically born with ink flowing through her veins:

> It is not singular that, as the daughter of two persons of distinguished literary celebrity, I should very early in life have thought of writing. . . . My husband . . . was from the first very anxious that I should prove myself worthy of my parentage and enroll myself on the page of fame.

In order to prove herself worthy of her parentage, Mary, paradoxically enough, must thus usurp the parental role and succeed in giving birth to *herself* on paper. Her declaration of existence as a writer must therefore figuratively repeat the matricide that her physical birth all too literally entailed. The connection between literary creation and the death of a parent is in fact suggested in the novel by the fact that, immediately after the monster's animation, Victor Frankenstein dreams that he holds the corpse of his dead mother in his arms. It is also suggested by the juxtaposition of two seemingly unrelated uses of italics in the novel: Mary's statement that she had *thought of a story* (which she inexplicably underlines twice) and the monster's promise to Frankenstein, *I will be with you on your wedding night*, which is repeatedly italicized. Both are eliminations of the mother, since the story Mary writes is a tale of motherless birth, and the wedding night marks the death of Frankenstein's bride, Elizabeth. Indeed, Mary herself was in fact the unwitting murderous intruder present on her own parents' wedding night: their decision to marry was due to the fact that Mary Wollstonecraft was already carrying the child that was to kill her. When Mary, describing her waking vision of catastrophic creation, affirms that "His success would terrify the artist," she is not giving vent to any ordinary fear-of-success syndrome. Or rather, what her book suggests is that what is at stake behind what is currently being banalized under the name of female fear of success is nothing less than the fear of somehow effecting the death of one's own parents.

It is not, however, the necessary murderousness of any declaration of female subjectivity that Mary Shelley's novel is proposing as its most troubling message of monsterdom. For, in a strikingly contemporary sort of predicament, Mary had not one but *two* mothers, each of whom consisted in the knowledge of the unviability of the other. After the death of Mary Wollstonecraft, Mary's father William Godwin married a woman as opposite in character and outlook as possible, a staunch housewifely mother of two who clearly preferred her own children to Godwin's. Between the courageous, passionate, intelligent, and suicidal mother Mary knew only through her writings and the vulgar, repressive "pustule of vanity" whose dislike she resented and returned, Mary must have known at first hand a whole gamut of feminine contradictions, impasses, and options. For the complexities of the demands, desires, and sufferings of Mary's life as a woman were staggering. Her father, who had once been a vehement opponent of the institution of marriage, nearly disowned his daughter for running away with Shelley, an already married disciple of Godwin's own former views. Shelley himself, who believed in multiple love objects, amicably fostered an erotic correspondence between Mary and his friend Thomas Jefferson Hogg, among others. For years, Mary and Shelley were accompanied everywhere by Mary's stepsister Claire, whom Mary did not particularly like, who had a child by Byron, and who maintained an ambiguous relation with Shelley. During the writing of *Frankenstein*, Mary learned of the suicide of her half sister Fanny Imlay, her mother's illegitimate child by an American lover, and the suicide of Shelley's wife Harriet, who was pregnant by a man other than Shelley. By the time she and Shelley married, Mary had had two children; she would have two more by the time of Shelley's death, and would watch as all but one of the children died in infancy. Widowed at age twenty-four, she never remarried. It is thus indeed perhaps the very hiddenness of the question of femininity in *Frankenstein* that somehow proclaims the painful message not of female monstrousness but of female contradictions. For it is the fact of self-contradiction that is so vigorously repressed in women. While the story of a man who is haunted by his own contradictions is representable as an allegory of monstrous doubles, how indeed would it have been possible for Mary to represent feminine contradiction *from the point of view of its repression* otherwise than precisely in the *gap* between angels of domesticity and an uncompleted monsteress, between the murdered Elizabeth and the dismembered Eve?

It is perhaps because the novel does succeed in conveying the unresolvable contradictions inherent in being female that Shelley himself felt compelled to write a prefatory disclaimer in Mary's name before he could let loose his wife's hideous progeny upon the world. In a series of denials jarringly at odds with the daring negativity of the novel, Shelley places the following words in Mary's mouth:

> I am by no means indifferent to the manner in which whatever moral tendencies exist in the sentiments or characters it contains shall affect the reader; yet my chief concern in this respect has been limited to . . . the exhibition of the amiableness of domestic affection, and the excellence of universal virtue. The opinions which naturally spring from the character and situation of the hero are by no means to be conceived as existing always in my own conviction; nor is any inference justly to be drawn from the following pages as prejudicing any philosophical doctrine of whatever kind.

How is this to be read except as a gesture of repression of the very specificity of the power of feminine contradiction, a gesture reminiscent of Frankenstein's destruction of his nearly-completed female monster? What is being repressed here is the possibility that a woman can write anything that would *not* exhibit "the amiableness of domestic affection," the possibility that for women as well as for men the home can be the very site of the *unheimlich*.

It can thus be seen in all three of the books we have discussed that the monstrousness of selfhood is intimately embedded within the question of female autobiography. Yet how could it be otherwise, since the very notion of a self, the very shape of human life stories, has always, from St. Augustine to Freud, been modeled on the man? Rousseau's—or any man's—autobiography consists precisely in the story of the difficulty of conforming to the standard of what a *man* should be. The problem for the female autobiographer is, on the one hand, to resist the pressure of masculine autobiography as the only literary genre available for her enterprise, and, on the other, to describe a difficulty in conforming to a female ideal which is largely a fantasy of the masculine, not the feminine, imagination. The fact that these three books deploy a *theory* of autobiography as monstrosity, within the framework of a less overtly avowed struggle with the raw materials of the authors' own lives and writing is perhaps, in the final analysis, precisely what is most autobiographically fertile and *telling* about them.

Frankenstein's Fallen Angel

Joyce Carol Oates

"Am I to be thought the only criminal, when all human kind sinned against me?"

FRANKENSTEIN'S DEMON

Quite apart from its enduring celebrity, and its proliferation in numberless extraliterary forms, Mary Shelley's *Frankenstein; or, The Modern Prometheus* is a remarkable work. A novel *sui generis*, if a novel at all, it is a unique blending of Gothic, fabulist, allegorical, and philosophical materials. Though certainly one of the most calculated and *willed* of fantasies, being in large part a kind of gloss upon or rejoinder to John Milton's *Paradise Lost*, *Frankenstein* is fueled by the kind of grotesque, faintly absurd, and wildly inventive images that spring direct from the unconscious: the eight-foot creature designed to be "beautiful," who turns out almost indescribably repulsive (yellow-skinned, shriveled of countenance, with straight black lips and near-colorless eyes); the cherished cousin-bride who *is* beautiful but, in the mind's dreaming, yields horrors ("As I imprinted the first kiss on her lips, they became livid with the hue of death; her features appeared to change, and I thought that I held the corpse of my dead mother in my arms; a shroud enveloped her form, and I saw the grave-worms crawling in the folds"); the mad dream of the Arctic as a country of "eternal light" that will prove, of course, only a place of endless ice, the appropriate landscape for Victor Frankenstein's death and his demon's self-immolation.

Central to *Frankenstein*—as it is central to a vastly different nineteenth-century romance, *Jane Eyre*—is a stroke of lightning that appears to issue in a dazzling "stream of fire" from a beautiful old oak tree ("So

---

From *Critical Inquiry* 10, no. 3 (March 1984). © 1984 by the University of Chicago.

soon the light vanished, the oak had disappeared, and nothing remained but a blasted stump"): the literal stimulus for Frankenstein's subsequent discovery of the cause of generation and life. And according to Mary Shelley's prefatory account of the origin of her "ghost story," the very image of Frankenstein and his demon-creature sprang from a waking dream of extraordinary vividness:

> I did not sleep, nor could I be said to think. My imagination, unbidden, possessed and guided me, gifting the successive images that arose in my mind with a vividness far beyond the usual bound of reverie. I saw—with shut eyes, but acute mental vision—I saw the pale student of unhallowed arts kneeling beside the thing he had put together. I saw the hideous phantasm of a man stretched out, and then, on the working of some powerful engine, show signs of life, and stir with an uneasy, half-vital motion. . . . The student sleeps: but he is awakened; he opens his eyes: behold the horrid thing stands at his bedside, opening his curtains, and looking on him with yellow, watery, but speculative eyes.

Hallucinatory and surrealist on its deepest level, *Frankenstein* is of course one of the most self-consciously literary "novels" ever written: its awkward form is the epistolary Gothic; its lyric descriptions of natural scenes (the grandiose Valley of Chamounix in particular) spring from Romantic sources; its speeches and monologues echo both Shakespeare and Milton; and, should the author's didactic intention not be clear enough, the demon-creature educates himself by studying three books of symbolic significance—Goethe's *Sorrows of Young Werther,* Plutarch's *Lives,* and Milton's *Paradise Lost.* (The last conveniently supplies him with a sense of his own predicament, as Mary Shelley hopes to dramatize it. He reads Milton's great epic as if it were a "true history" giving the picture of an omnipotent God warring with His creatures; he identifies himself with Adam, except so far as Adam had come forth from God a "perfect creature, happy and prosperous." Finally, of course, he identifies with Satan: "I am thy creature: I ought to be thy Adam; but I am rather the fallen angel, whom thou drivest from joy for no misdeed. Everywhere I see bliss, from which I alone am irrevocably excluded. I was benevolent and good; misery made me a fiend. Make me happy, and I shall again be virtuous.")

The search of medieval alchemists for the legendary philosophers' stone (the talismanic process by which base metals might be transformed into gold or, in psychological terms, the means by which the individual might realize his destiny), Faust's reckless defiance of human limitations and his willingness to barter his soul for knowledge, the fatal search of such tragic figures as Oedipus and Hamlet for answers to the mysteries of their lives—these are the archetypal dramas to which *Frankenstein* bears an obvious kinship. Yet, as one reads, as Frankenstein and his despised shadow-self engage in one after another of the novel's many dialogues, it begins to seem as if the nineteen-year-old author is discovering these archetypal elements for the first time. Frankenstein "is" a demonic parody (or extension) of Milton's God; he "is" *Prometheus plasticator,* the creator of mankind; but at the same time, by his own account, he is totally unable to control the behavior of his demon (variously called "monster," "fiend," "wretch," but necessarily lacking a name). Surprisingly, it is not by way of the priggish and "self-devoted" young scientist that Mary Shelley discovers the great power of her narrative but by way of the misshapen demon, with whom most readers identify: "My person was hideous, and my stature gigantic: What did this mean? Who was I? What was I? Whence did I come? What was my destination? It is not simply the case that the demon—like Satan and Adam in *Paradise Lost*—has the most compelling speeches in the novel and is far wiser and more magnanimous than his creator: he is also the means by which a transcendent love—a romantically *unrequited love*—is expressed. Surely one of the secrets of *Frankenstein,* which helps to account for its abiding appeal, is the demon's patient, unquestioning, utterly faithful, and utterly *human* love for his irresponsible creator.

When Frankenstein is tracking the demon into the Arctic regions, for instance, it is clearly the demon who is helping him in his search, and even leaving food for him; but Frankenstein is so blind—in fact so comically blind—he believes that "spirits" are responsible. "Yet still a spirit of good followed and directed my steps, and, when I most murmured, would suddenly extricate me from seemingly insurmountable difficulties. Sometimes, when nature, overcome by hunger, sunk under the exhaustion, a repast was prepared for me in the desert, that restored and inspirited me. . . . I may not doubt that it was set there by the spirits that I had invoked to aid me."

By degrees, with the progression of the fable's unlikely plot, the inhuman creation becomes increasingly human while his creator becomes increasingly inhuman, frozen in a posture of rigorous denial.

(*He* is blameless of any wrongdoing in terms of the demon and even dares to tell Walton, literally with his dying breath, that another scientist might succeed where he had failed!—the lesson of the "Frankenstein monster" is revealed as totally lost on Frankenstein himself.) The demon is (sub)human consciousness-in-the-making, naturally benevolent as Milton's Satan is not, and received with horror and contempt solely because of his physical appearance. He is sired without a mother in defiance of nature, but he is in one sense an infant—a comically monstrous eight-foot baby—whose progenitor rejects him immediately after creating him, in one of the most curious (and dreamlike) scenes in the novel:

> "How can I describe my emotions at this catastrophe, or how delineate the wretch whom, with such infinite pains and care, I had endeavored to form? . . . I had worked hard for nearly two years, for the sole purpose of infusing life into an inanimate body. For this I had deprived myself of rest and health. I had desired it with an ardor that far exceeded moderation; but now that I had finished, the beauty of the dream vanished, and breathless horror and disgust filled my heart. Unable to endure the aspect of the being I had created, I rushed out of the room, and continued a long time traversing my bed-chamber, unable to compose my mind to sleep."

Here follows the nightmare vision of Frankenstein's bride-to-be, Elizabeth, as a form of his dead mother, with "grave-worms crawling" in her shroud; and shortly afterward the "wretch" himself appears at Frankenstein's bed, drawing away the canopy as Mary Shelley had imagined. But Frankenstein is so cowardly he runs away again; and this time the demon is indeed abandoned, to reappear only after the first of the "murders" of Frankenstein's kin. On the surface, Frankenstein's behavior is preposterous, even idiotic, for he seems blind to the fact that is apparent to any reader—that he has loosed a fearful power into the world, whether it strikes his eye as aesthetically pleasing or not, and he *must* take responsibility for it. Except, of course, he does not. For, as he keeps telling himself, he is blameless of any wrongdoing apart from the act of creation itself. The emotions he catalogs for us—gloom, sorrow, misery, despair—are conventionally Romantic attitudes, mere luxuries in a context that requires *action* and not simply *response*.

By contrast the demon is all activity, all yearning, all hope. His love for his maker is unrequited and seems incapable of making any impression upon Frankenstein; yet the demon never gives it up, even when he sounds most threatening: "Beware," says the demon midway in the novel, "for I am fearless, and therefore powerful. I will watch with the wiliness of a snake, that I may sting with its venom. Man, you shall repent of the injuries you inflict." His voice is very like his creator's—indeed, everyone in *Frankenstein* sounds alike—but his posture is always one of simple need: he requires love in order to become less monstrous, but, as he *is* a monster, love is denied him; and the man responsible for this comically tragic state of affairs says repeatedly that he is not to blame. Frankenstein's typical response to the situation is: "I felt as if I had committed some great crime, the consciousness of which haunted me. I was guiltless, but I had indeed drawn a horrible curse upon my head, as mortal as that of crime." But if Frankenstein is not to blame for the various deaths that occur, who is? Had he endowed his creation, as God endowed Adam in Milton's epic, with free will? Or is the demon psychologically his creature, committing the forbidden acts Frankenstein wants committed?—so long as Frankenstein himself remains "guiltless."

It is a measure of the subtlety of this moral parable that the demon strikes so many archetypal chords and suggests so many variant readings. He recapitulates in truncated form the history of consciousness of his race (learning to speak, read, write, etc., by closely watching the De Lacey family); he is an abandoned child, a parentless orphan; he takes on the voices of Adam, Satan ("Evil thenceforth became my good," he says, as Milton's fallen angel says, "Evil be thou my good"), even our "first mother," Eve. When the demon terrifies himself by seeing his reflection in a pool, and grasping at once the nature of his own deformity, he is surely not mirroring Narcissus, as some commentators have suggested, but Milton's Eve in her surprised discovery of her own beauty, in book 4 of *Paradise Lost:*

> I thither went
> With unexperienc't thought, and laid me down
> On the green bank, to look into the clear
> Smooth Lake, that to me seem'd another Sky.
> As I bent down to look, just opposite,
> A Shape within the wat'ry gleam appear'd
> Bending to look on me, I started back,

It started back, but pleas'd I soon return'd,
Pleas'd it return'd as soon with answering looks
Of sympathy and love; there I had fixt
Mine eyes till now, and pin'd with vain desire.
(ll. 456–66)

He is Shakespeare's Edmund, though *unloved*—a shadow figure more tragic, because more "conscious," than the hero he represents. Most suggestively, he has become by the novel's melodramatic conclusion a form of Christ: sinned against by all humankind, yet fundamentally blameless, and *yet* quite willing to die as a sacrifice. He speaks of his death as a "consummation"; he is going to burn himself on a funeral pyre somewhere in the Arctic wastes—unlikely, certainly, but a fitting end to a life conceived by way of lightning and electricity:

> "But soon," he cried with sad and solemn enthusiasm, "I shall die, and what I now feel be no longer felt. Soon these burning miseries will be extinct. I shall ascend my funeral pile triumphantly, and exult in the agony of the torturing flames. The light of that conflagration will fade away; my ashes will be swept into the sea by the winds. My spirit will sleep in peace; or, if it thinks, it will not surely think thus."

But the demon does not die within the confines of the novel, so perhaps he has not died after all. He is, in the end, a "modern" species of shadow or *Doppelgänger—the nightmare that is deliberately created by man's ingenuity* and not a mere supernatural being of fairy-tale remnant.

Frankenstein's double significance as a work of prose fiction and a cultural myth—as "novel" of 1818 and timeless "metaphor"—makes it a highly difficult story to read directly. A number of popular misconceptions obscure it for most readers: Frankenstein is of course *not* the monster, but his creator; nor is he a mad scientist of genius—he is in fact a highly idealistic and naïve youth in the conventional Romantic mode (in Walton's admiring eyes, "noble," "cultivated," a "celestial spirit" who has suffered "great and unparalleled misfortunes"), not unlike Mary Shelley's fated lover Shelley. Despite the fact that a number of catastrophes occur around him and indirectly because of him, Victor Frankenstein is well intentioned, gentlemanly, *good*. He is no sadist like H. G. Wells's exiled vivisectionist Dr. Moreau, who boasts: "You cannot imagine the strange colorless delight of these intellectual desires. The thing before you is no longer an animal, a fellow-creature, but a problem." Frankenstein's mission, on the other hand, is selfless, even messianic:

> "No one can conceive the variety of feelings which bore me onwards, like a hurricane, in the first enthusiasm of success. Life and death appeared to me ideal bounds, which I should first break through, and pour a torrent of light into our dark world. A new species would bless me as its creator and source; many happy and excellent natures would owe their being to me. No father could claim the gratitude of his child so completely as I should deserve theirs. . . . If I could bestow animation upon lifeless matter, I might in the process of time . . . renew life where death had apparently devoted the body to corruption."

It is a measure of the novel's extraordinary fame that the very name "Frankenstein" has long since supplanted "Prometheus" in popular usage; and the Frankenstein legend retains a significance for our time as the Prometheus legend does not.

How many fictional characters, after all, have made the great leap from literature to mythology? How many creations of sheer language have stepped from the rhythms of their authors' idiosyncratic voices into what might be called a collective cultural consciousness? Don Quixote, Dracula, Sherlock Holmes, Alice (in Wonderland), certain figures in the fairy tales of Hans Christian Andersen . . . and of course Frankenstein's "monster." Virtually millions of people who have never heard of the novel *Frankenstein*, let alone that a young Englishwoman named Mary Shelley (in fact Godwin) wrote it at the age of nineteen, are well acquainted with the image of Frankenstein popularized by Boris Karloff in the 1930s and understand, at least intuitively, the ethical implications of the metaphor. (As in the expression, particularly relevant for our time, "We have created a Frankenstein monster.") The more potent the archetype evoked by a work of literature, the more readily its specific form slips free of the time-bound *personal* work. On the level of cultural myth, the figures of Dracula, Sherlock Holmes, Alice, and the rest are near-autonomous beings, linked to no specific books and no specific authors. They have become communal creations; they belong to us all. Hence the very real difficulty in reading Mary

Shelley's novel for the first time. (Subsequent readings are far easier and yield greater rewards.)

Precisely because of this extraordinary fame, one should be reminded of how original and unique the novel was at the time of its publication. Can it even be read at the present time in a context hospitable to its specific allusions and assumptions—one conversant with the thorny glories of *Paradise Lost*, the sentimental ironies of Coleridge's "Rime of the Ancient Mariner," the Gothic conventions of tales-within-tales, epistolary frames, and histrionic speeches delivered at length? In a more accomplished work, *Wuthering Heights*, the structural complexities of tales-within-tales are employed for artistic ends: the ostensible fracturing of time yields a rich poetic significance; characters grow and change like people whom we have come to know. In Mary Shelley's *Frankenstein* the strained conventions of the romance are mere structural devices to allow Victor Frankenstein and his demon their opposing—but intimately linked—"voices." Thus, abrupt transitions in space and time take place in a kind of rhetorical vacuum: all is summary, past history, *exemplum*.

But it is a mistake to read *Frankenstein* as a modern novel of psychological realism, or as a "novel" at all. It contains no characters, only points of view; its concerns are pointedly moral and didactic; it makes no claims for verisimilitude of even a poetic Wordsworthian nature. (The Alpine landscapes are all self-consciously sublime and theatrical; Mont Blanc, for instance, suggests "another earth, the habitations of another race of beings.") If one were pressed to choose a literary antecedent for *Frankenstein*, it might be, surprisingly, Samuel Johnson's *Rasselas*, rather than a popular Gothic work like Mrs. Radcliffe's *Mysteries of Udolpho*, which allegedly had the power to frighten its readers. (A character in Jane Austen's *Northanger Abbey* says of this once famous novel: "I remember finishing it in two days—my hair standing on end the whole time.") Though *Frankenstein* and *Dracula* are commonly linked, Bram Stoker's tour de force of 1897 is vastly different in tone, theme, and intention from Mary Shelley's novel: its "monster" is not at all monstrous in appearance, only in behavior; and he is thoroughly and irremediably evil by nature. But no one in *Frankenstein* is evil—the universe is emptied of God and of theistic assumptions of "good" and "evil." Hence, its modernity.

Tragedy does not arise spontaneous and unwilled in so "modern" a setting; it must be made—in fact, manufactured. The Fates are not to blame; there *are* no Fates, only the brash young scientist who boasts of never having feared the supernatural. ("In my education my father had taken the greatest precautions that my mind should be impressed with no supernatural horrors. I do not ever remember to have trembled at a tale of superstition, or to have feared the apparition of a spirit. . . . A churchyard was to me merely the receptacle of bodies deprived of life, which, from being the seat of beauty and strength, had become food for the worm.") Where *Dracula* and other conventional Gothic works are fantasies, with clear links to fairy tales and legends, and even popular ballads, *Frankenstein* has the theoretical and cautionary tone of science fiction. It is meant to prophesy, not to entertain.

Another aspect of *Frankenstein's* uniqueness lies in the curious bond between Frankenstein and his created demon. Where, by tradition, such beings as doubles, shadow-selves, "imps of the perverse," and classic *Doppelgängers* (like poor Golyadkin's nemesis in Dostoyevski's *Double* [1846]) spring full grown from supernatural origins—that is, from unacknowledged recesses of the human spirit—Frankenstein's demon is *natural* in origin: a manufactured nemesis. He is an abstract idea made flesh, a Platonic essence given a horrific (and certainly ludicrous) existence. Yet though he is meant to be Frankenstein's ideal, a man-made miracle that would "pour a torrent of light into our dark world," he is only a fragment of that ideal—which is to say, a mockery, a parody, a joke. The monsters we create by way of an advanced technological civilization "are" ourselves as we cannot hope to see ourselves—incomplete, blind, blighted, and, most of all, self-destructive. For it is the forbidden wish for death that dominates. (In intention it is customarily the deaths of others, "enemies"; in fact it may be our own deaths we plan.) Hence the tradition of recognizing Faustian pacts with the devil as acts of aggression against the human self—the very "I" of the rational being.

Since Frankenstein's creature is made up of parts collected from charnel houses and graves and his creator acknowledges that he "disturbed, with profane fingers, the tremendous secrets of the human frame," it is inevitable that the creature be a *profane* thing. He cannot be blessed or loved: he springs not from a natural union but has been forged in what Frankenstein calls a "workshop of filthy creation." One of the brilliant surrealist touches of the narrative is that Frankenstein's shadow-self is a giant; even the rationalization for this curious decision is ingenious. "As the minuteness of the parts formed a great hindrance to my speed," Frankenstein explains to Walton, "I resolved, contrary to my first intention, to make the being of a gigantic stature; that is to say, about eight feet in height, and proportionably large." A demon of mere human size would not have been nearly so compelling.

(The reader should keep in mind that, in 1818, the notion that "life" might be galvanized in laboratory conditions was really not so farfetched, for the properties of electricity were not commonly understood and seem to have been bound up magically with what might be called metaphorically the "spark" of life. Again, in 1984, the possibility of artificially induced life, human or otherwise, does not seem especially remote.)

Because in one sense the demon *is* Frankenstein's deepest self, the relationship between them is dreamlike, fraught with undefined emotion. Throughout the novel Frankenstein is susceptible to fainting fits, bouts of illness and exhaustion, and nightmares of romantic intensity—less a fully realized personality than a queer stunted half-self (rather like Roderick Usher, whose sister Madeleine, *his* secret self, is buried alive). It is significant that as soon as Frankenstein induces life in his eight-foot monster, he notices *for the first time* what he has created. "His limbs were in proportion," Frankenstein testifies, "and I had selected his features as beautiful." But something has clearly gone wrong:

> "Beautiful! Great God! His yellow skin scarcely covered the work of muscles and arteries beneath; his hair was of lustrous black, and flowing; his teeth of a pearly whiteness; but these luxuriances only formed a more horrid contrast with his watery eyes, that seemed almost of the same color as the dun white sockets in which they were set, his shrivelled complexion, and straight black lips."

Significant too is the fact that Frankenstein retreats from this vision and falls asleep—an unlikely response in naturalistic terms but quite appropriate symbolically—so that, shortly afterward, his demon can arouse *him* from sleep:

> "I started from my sleep with horror; a cold dew covered my forehead, my teeth chattered, and every limb became convulsed; when, by the dim and yellow light of the moon, as it forced its way through the window-shutters, I beheld the wretch, the miserable monster whom I had created. He held up the curtain of the bed; and his eyes, if eyes they may be called, were fixed on me. His jaws opened, and he

mutterd some inarticulate sounds, while a grin wrinkled his cheeks."

"Oh! no mortal could support the horror of that counte-nance. A mummy again endued with animation could not be so hideous as that wretch. I had gazed on him while unfinished; he was ugly then; but when those muscles and joints were rendered capable of motion, it became a thing such as Dante could not have conceived."

Frankenstein's superficial response to the "thing" he has created is solely in aesthetic terms, for his atheistic morality precludes all thoughts of transgression. (Considering that the author of *Frankenstein* is a woman, a woman well acquainted with pregnancy and childbirth at a precocious age, it is curious that nowhere in the novel does anyone raise the issue of the demon's "unnatural" genesis: he is a monster-son born of Man exclusively, a parody of the Word or the Idea made Flesh.) Ethically, Frankenstein is "blameless"—though he is haunted by the suspicion throughout that he has committed a crime of some sort, with the very best of intentions.

Where the realistic novel presents characters in a more or less coherent "field," as part of a defined society, firmly established in time and place, romance does away with questions of verisimilitude and plausibility altogether and deals directly with the elements of narrative: it might be said to be an "easier" form psychologically, since it evokes archetypal responses on its primary level. No one expects Victor Frankenstein to behave plausibly when he is a near-allegorical figure; no one expects his demon to behave plausibly since he *is* a demonic presence, an outsized mirror image of his creator. When the demon warns Frankenstein (in traditional Gothic form, incidentally), "*I shall be with you on your wedding night,*" it seems only natural, granted Frankenstein's egocentricity, that he worry about his own safety and not his bride's and that, despite the warning, Frankenstein allows Elizabeth to be murdered. His wish is his demon-self's command, though he never acknowledges his complicity. Indeed, *Frankenstein* begins to read as an antiromance, a merciless critique of Romantic attitudes—sorrow, misery, self-loathing, despair, paralysis, etc.—written, as it were, from the inside, by a young woman who had already lost a baby in infancy (in 1815, a girl), would lose another, also a girl, in 1817, and, in 1819, lost a third—named, oddly, William (the very name of the little boy murdered early in the narrative by Frankenstein's demon). Regardless of the sufferings of others, the romantically "self-devoted" hero responds solely in terms of his own emotions. He might be a lyric poet of the early 1800s, for all his preoccupation with self: everything refers tragically to him; everything is rendered in terms of *his* experience:

> Great God! Why did I not then expire? Why am I here to relate the destruction of the best hope, and the purest creature of earth? [Elizabeth] was there, lifeless and inanimate, thrown across the bed, her head hanging down, and her pale and distorted features half covered by her hair. Everywhere I turn I see the same figure,—her bloodless arms and relaxed form flung by the murderer on its bridal bier. Could I behold this, and live? (Alas, life is obstinate, and clings closest where it is most hated.) For a moment only, and I lost recollection: I fainted.

Frankenstein grapples with the complex moral issues raised by his demonic creation by "fainting" in one way or another throughout the novel. And in his abrogation of consciousness and responsibility, the demon naturally acts: for this *is* the Word, the secret wish for destruction, made Flesh.

The cruelest act of all is performed by Frankenstein before the very eyes of his demon: this is the sudden destruction of the partly assembled "bride." He makes the creature at the bidding of his demon, who has promised, most convincingly, to leave Europe with her and to live "virtuously"; but, suddenly repulsed by the "filthy process" he has undertaken, Frankenstein destroys his work. ("The wretch saw me destroy the creature on whose future existence he depended for happiness, and with a howl of devilish despair and revenge, withdrew.") Afterward he thinks, looking at the remains of the half-finished creature, that he has *almost* mangled the living flesh of a human being; but he never feels any remorse for what he has done and never considers that, in "mangling" the flesh of his demon's bride, he is murdering the pious and rather too perfect Elizabeth, the cousin-bride whom he professes to love. "Am I to be thought the only criminal," the demon asks, "when all human kind sinned against me?" He might have said as reasonably, *when all humankind conspired in my sin.*

While *Paradise Lost* is to Frankenstein's demon (and very likely to Mary Shelley as well) the picture of an "omnipotent God warring with his creatures," *Frankenstein* is the picture of a finite and flawed god at war with, and eventually overcome by, his creation. It is a parable for our time, an enduring prophecy, a remarkably acute diagnosis of the lethal nature of *denial:* denial of responsibility for one's actions, denial of the shadow-self locked within consciousness. Even in the debased and sensational form in which Frankenstein's monster is known by most persons—as a kind of retarded giant, one might say, with electrodes in his neck—his archetypal significance rings true. "My form," he says eloquently, "is a filthy type of yours."

"My Hideous Progeny": The Lady and the Monster

Mary Poovey

Numerous critics have commented on Mary Shelley's complicated relationship with her remarkable literary family. Her brief, secret courtship with Percy Shelley was largely conducted in St. Pancras's Churchyard, where Mary took her books to read beside her mother's grave; she read and reread the works of both her father and her mother while she was growing up; and her letters to Percy show an ongoing concern both with his works and with her own. Two less easily documentable considerations are equally important for the light they shed on Mary's attitude toward her family of authors. The first is that much of what she read must have alternately sanctioned and condemned her adolescent ambition and thus served to enhance the ambivalence she was to continue to display toward any kind of personal assertion. Reading Wollstonecraft's *Maria* and *The Rights of Woman*, Godwin's *Memoirs* of her mother or his *Political Justice*, undoubtedly provided intellectual justification for Mary Shelley's defiance of social values. Yet, even before Godwin's angry reprisal, she must have anticipated that polite society, at the very least, would judge her unusual conduct harshly; for the public response to her mother's *Memoirs*, in which Godwin revealed Wollstonecraft's affair with Imlay and the illegitimacy of her daughter Fanny, had been almost universally abusive, and Mary Godwin had now committed virtually the same "crime." The second important consideration about Mary Shelley's relationship to her fam-

From *The Proper Lady and the Woman Writer.* © 1984 by the University of Chicago. Unversity of Chicago Press, 1984.

ily is that, at least in retrospect, she felt extreme pressure to measure up to the standards they set. In her 1831 introduction to *Frankenstein*, Shelley records the expectations that, more than a decade later, constituted some of her most vivid memories of her young adulthood. "My husband . . . was from the first, very anxious that I should prove myself worthy of my parentage, and enrol myself on the page of fame. He was for ever inciting me to obtain literary reputation." This injunction—not only to write but to "obtain literary reputation" —reinforced Shelley's persistent association of writing with an aggressive quest for public notice. Moreover, the expectation she sensed in her most intimate companion and projected onto herself, perhaps from the example of her parents, continued to drive Mary Shelley to develop a self-definition based at least in part on the assertive activity of professional writing.

When she was in Switzerland in the summer of 1816, Mary Shelley's creative energies were finally rerouted from "travelling, and the cares of family" to this all-important activity of writing. Living next to Lord Byron, listening to—thought not participating in—the conversations of the two poets ("incapacity and timidity always prevented my mingling in the nightly conversations," she said, and no doubt inspired by Percy's example, Mary Shelley began to compose steadily. After July 24, 1816, her journal frequently contains the important monosyllable, "Write," and the attention Percy devoted to the novel's progress, its revisions, and, eventually, its publication reveals that his support for the project was as enthusiastic as Mary could have wished. But the narrative that Mary Shelley wrote between that "eventful" summer and the following April was less a wholehearted celebration of the imaginative enterprise she had undertaken in order to prove her worth to Percy than a troubled, veiled exploration of the price she had already begun to fear such egotistical self-assertion might exact. *Frankenstein* occupies a particularly important place in Shelley's career, not only because it is by far her most famous work, but because, in 1831, she prepared significant revisions and an important introduction, both of which underscore and elaborate her initial ambivalence. By tracing first the contradictions already present in the 1813 edition and then the revisions she made after Percy's death and her return to England, we can begin to see the roots and progress of Shelley's growing desire to accommodate her adolescent impulses to conventional propriety. Taken together, the two editions of *Frankenstein* provide a case study of the tensions inherent in the confrontation between the expectations Shelley associated, on the one hand, with her mother and Romantic originality and, on the other, with a textbook Proper Lady.

THE 1818 *FRANKENSTEIN*

Even though they praised the power and stylistic vigor of *Frankenstein*, its first reviewers sharply criticized the anonymous novelist's failure to moralize about the novel's startling, even blasphemous, subject. The reviewer for the *Quarterly Review*, for example, complained that

> Our taste and our judgment alike revolt at this kind of writing, and the greater the ability with which it may be executed the worse it is—it inculcates no lesson of conduct, manners, or morality; it cannot mend, and will not even amuse its readers, unless their taste have been deplorably vitiated—it fatigues the feelings without interesting the understanding; it gratuitously harasses the heart, and only adds to the store, already too great, of painful sensations.

Presumably because it was unthinkable that a woman should refuse to moralize, most critics automatically assumed that the author of *Frankenstein* was a man—no doubt a "follower of Godwin," according to *Blackwood's*, or even Percy Shelley himself, as the *Edinburgh Magazine* surmised. These reviewers, however, were too preoccupied with the explicit unorthodoxy of *Frankenstein*'s subject to attend carefully to the undercurrents in it that challenged their opinion. Like her mother and many male Romantics, Mary Shelley had chosen to focus on the theme of Promethean desire, which has implications for both the development of culture and the individual creative act; but when *Frankenstein* is considered alongside contemporary works that display even some degree of confidence in imaginative power, it proves to be more conservative than her first readers realized. Indeed, *Frankenstein* calls into question, not the social conventions that inhibit creativity, but rather the egotism that Mary Shelley associates with the artist's monstrous self-assertion.

Like Wollstonecraft and most male Romantics, Shelley discusses desire explicitly within a paradigm of individual maturation: *Frankenstein* is Shelley's version of the process of identity-formation that Wollstonecraft worked out in her two *Vindications*. Keats called this maturation "soul-making," and Wordsworth devoted his longest completed poem to it. In the 1818 text, Shelley's model of maturation begins with a realistic depiction of Lockean psychology; young Victor Frankenstein is a *tabula rasa* whose character is formed by his childhood experiences. The son of loving, protective parents, the companion of affectionate friends, he soon finds the harmony of his childhood violated by what he calls a "predilection" for natural philosophy. Yet even though this "predilection" seems to be innate, Frankenstein locates its origin not in his own disposition but in a single childhood event—the accidental discovery of a volume of Cornelius Agrippa's occult speculations. The "fatal impulse" this volume sparks is then kindled into passionate enthusiasm by other accidents: Frankenstein's father neglects to explain Agrippa's obsolescence, a discussion provoked by a lightning bolt undermines his belief in the occult, and "some accident" prevents him from attending lectures on natural philosophy. Left with a craving for knowledge but no reliable guide to direct it, Frankenstein's curiosity is kept within bounds only by the "mutual affection" of his domestic circle.

In this dramatization of Victor Frankenstein's childhood, Mary Shelley fuses mechanistic psychological theories of the origin and development of character with the more organic theories generally associated with the Romantics. Like most contemporary Lockean philosophers, she asserts that circumstances activate and direct an individual's capacity for imaginative activity; the inclination or predilection thus formed then constitutes the basis of identity. But when Shelley combines this model with the notion (implied by Wollstonecraft's *Letters Written . . . in Sweden* and by the poetry of Wordsworth, Coleridge, Byron, and Percy Shelley) that an individual's desire, once aroused, has its own impetus and logic, she comes up with a model of maturation that contradicts the optimism of both mechanists and organicists. More in keeping with eighteenth-century moralists than with either William Godwin or Percy Shelley, Mary Shelley characterizes innate desire not as neutral or benevolent but as quintessentially egotistical. And, unlike Mary Wollstonecraft, she does not conceive of imaginative activity as leading through intimations of mortality to new insight or creativity. Instead, she sees imagination as an appetite that can and must be regulated—specifically, by the give-and-take of domestic relationships. If it is aroused but is not controlled by human society, it will project itself into the natural world, becoming voracious in its search for objects to conquer and consume. This principle, which draws both mechanistic and organic models under the mantle of conventional warnings to women, constitutes the major dynamic of *Frankenstein*'s plot. As long as domestic relationships govern an individual's affections, his or her desire will turn outward as love. But when the individual loses or leaves the regulating influence of relationship with others, imaginative energy always threatens to turn back on itself, to "mark" all external objects as its own and to degenerate into "gloomy and narrow reflections upon self."

Shelley's exposition of the degeneration of incipient curiosity into full-fledged egotism begins when Frankenstein leaves his childhood home for the University of Ingolstadt. At the university he is left to "form [his] own friends, and be [his] own protector," and, given this freedom, his imagination is liberated to follow its natural course. To the young scholar, this energy seems well directed, for Frankenstein assumes that his ambition to conquer death through science is fundamentally unselfish. With supreme self-confidence, he "penetrate[s] into the recesses of nature" in search of the secret of life. What he discovers in the "vaults and charnel houses" he visits, however, is not life but death, the "natural decay and corruption of the human body." In pursuing his ambition even beyond this grisly sight, Frankenstein proves unequivocally that his "benevolent" scheme actually acts out the imagination's essential and deadly self-devotion. For what he really wants is not to serve others but to assert himself. Indeed, he wants ultimately to defy mortality, to found a "new species" that would "bless [him] as its creator and source." "No father could claim the gratitude of his child so completely as I should deserve their's," he boasts.

Frankenstein's particular vision of immortality and the vanity that it embodies have profound social consequences, both because Frankenstein would deny relationships (and women) any role in the conception of children and because he would reduce all domestic ties to those that center on and feed his selfish desires. Given the egotism of his ambition, it comes as no surprise that Frankenstein's love for his family is the first victim of his growing obsession; "supernatural enthusiasm" usurps the place of his previous domestic love. "I wished, as it were, to procrastinate all that related to my feelings of affection until the great object, which swallowed up every habit of my nature, should be completed." Frankenstein isolates himself in a "solitary chamber," refuses to write even to his fiancée, Elizabeth, and grows "insensible to the charms of nature." "I became as timid as a love-sick girl," he realizes, in retrospect, "and alternate tremor and passionate ardour took the place of wholesome sensation and regulated ambition."

Despite what the reviewers thought, in her dramatization of the imaginative quest Mary Shelley is actually more concerned with this antisocial dimension than with its metaphysical implications. In chapter 5, for example, at the heart of her story, she elaborates the significance of Frankenstein's self-absorption primarily in terms of his social relationships. After animating the monster, product and symbol of self-serving desire, Frankenstein falls asleep, only to dream the true meaning of his accomplishment: having denied domestic relationships by indulging his selfish passions, he has, in effect, murdered domestic tranquillity.

> I thought I saw Elizabeth, in the bloom of health, walking in the streets of Ingolstadt. Delighted and surprised, I embraced her; but as I imprinted the first kiss on her lips, they became livid with the hue of death; her features appeared to change, and I thought that I held the corpse of my dead mother in my arms; a shroud enveloped her form, and I saw the grave-worms crawling in the folds of the flannel.

Lover and mother, as the presiding female guardians of Frankenstein's "secluded and domestic" youth, are conflated in this tableau of the enthusiast's guilt. Only now, when Frankenstein starts from his sleep to find the misshapen creature hanging over his bed (as he himself will later hang over Elizabeth's) does he recognize his ambition for what it really is: a monstrous urge, alien and threatening to all human intercourse.

In effect, animating the monster completes and liberates Frankenstein's egotism, for his indescribable experiment gives explicit and autonomous form to his ambition and desire. Paradoxically, in this incident Shelley makes the ego's destructiveness literal by setting in motion the figurative, symbolic character of the monster. We will see later the significance of this event for the monster; for Frankenstein, this moment, which aborts his maturation, has the dual effect of initiating self-consciousness and, tragically, perfecting his alienation. Momentarily "restored to life" by his childhood friend Clerval, Frankenstein rejects the "selfish pursuit [that] had cramped and narrowed" him and returns his feeling to its proper objects, his "beloved friends." But ironically, the very gesture that disciplines his desire has already destroyed the possibility of reestablishing relationships with his loved ones. Liberating the monster allows Frankenstein to see that personal fulfillment results from self-denial rather than self-assertion, but it also condemns him to perpetual isolation and, therefore, to permanent incompleteness.

This fatal paradox, the heart of Mary Shelley's waking nightmare, gives a conventionally "feminine" twist to the argument that individuals mature through imaginative projection, confrontation, and self-consciousness. In the version of maturation that Wollstonecraft sketched out in her two *Vindications* and in *Letters Written . . . in Sweden* and that Wordsworth set out more fully in *The Prelude*, the child's innate desires, stirred and nurtured by the mother's love, are soon projected outward toward the natural world. Desire takes this aggressive turn because in maternal love and in the receptivity this love cultivates "there exists / A virtue which irradiates and exalts / All objects through all intercourse of sense" (1805 *Prelude*, book 2, lines 258–60). As a result of both the child's growing confidence in the beneficence of the questing imagination and nature's generous response, the child is able to effect a radical break with the mother without suffering irretrievable loss.

> No outcast he, bewildered and depressed;
> Along his infant veins are interfused
> The gravitation and the filial bond
> Of Nature that connect him with the world.
> (*Prelude*, 2.261–64)

The heightened images of the self cast back from nature then help the child internalize a sense of autonomous identity and personal power.

In marked contrast, Mary Shelley distrusts both the imagination *and* the natural world. The imagination, as it is depicted in Frankenstein's original transgression, is incapable of projecting an irradiating virtue, for, in aiding and abetting the ego, the imagination expands the individual's self-absorption to fill the entire universe, and, as it does so, it murders everyone in its path. In *Frankenstein*, the monster simply acts out the implicit content of Frankenstein's desire: just as Frankenstein figuratively murdered his family, so the monster literally murders Frankenstein's domestic relationships, blighting both the memory and the hope of domestic harmony with the "black mark" of its deadly hand. William Frankenstein, Justine Moritz, Henry Clerval, even Elizabeth Lavenza are, as it were, literally *possessed* by this creature; but, as Frankenstein knows all too well, its victims are by extension his own:

Justine is *his* "unhappy victim"; *he* has murdered Clerval; and the creature consummates *his* deadly desire on "*its* bridal bier."

By the same token, Mary Shelley also distrusts nature, for, far from curbing the imagination, nature simply encourages imaginative projection. Essentially, Mary Shelley's understanding of nature coincides with those of Wordsworth, Wollstonecraft, and Percy Shelley. But where these three trust the imagination to disarm the natural world of its meaninglessness by projecting human content into it, Mary Shelley's anxiety about the imagination bleeds into the world it invades. In the inhospitable world most graphically depicted in the final setting of *Frankenstein*, nature is "terrifically desolate," frigid, and fatal to human beings and human relationships. These fields of ice provide a fit home only for the monster, that incarnation of the imagination's ugly and deadly essence.

Thus Shelley does not depict numerous natural theaters into which the individual can project his or her growing desire and from which affirmative echoes will return to hasten the process of maturation. Instead, she continues to dramatize personal fulfillment strictly in terms of the child's original domestic harmony, with the absent mother now replaced by the closest female equivalent: ideally, Elizabeth would link Frankenstein's maturity to his youth, just as Mrs. Saville should anchor the mariner Walton. Ideally, in other words, the beloved object would be sought and found only within the comforting confines of preexisting domestic relationships. In this model, Shelley therefore ties the formation of personal identity to self-denial rather than self-assertion; personal identity for her entails defining oneself in terms of relationships (not one but many)—not, as Wollstonecraft and Wordsworth would have it, in terms of self-assertion, confrontation, freedom, and faith in the individualistic imaginative act.

Shelley repeatedly stresses the fatal kinship between the human imagination, nature, and death by the tropes of natural violence that describe all kinds of desire. Passion is like nature internalized, as even Frankenstein knows:

> When I would account to myself for the birth of that passion, which afterwards ruled my destiny, I find it arise, like a mountain river, from ignoble and almost forgotten sources; but, swelling, as it proceeded, it became the torrent which, in its course, has swept away all my hopes and joys.

Ambition drives Frankenstein "like a hurricane" as he engineers the monster and, after its liberation, he is a "blasted tree," utterly destroyed" by a lightning blast to his soul. Through these metaphoric associations, Shelley is laying the groundwork for the pattern acted out by the monster. *Like* forces in the natural world, Frankenstein's unregulated desire gathers strength until it erupts in the monster's creation; then the creature actualizes, externalizes, the pattern of nature— Frankenstein's nature and the natural world, now explicitly combined— with a power that destroys all society. In other words, the pattern inherent in the natural world and figuratively ascribed to the individual becomes, through the monster, Frankenstein's literal "fate" or "destiny."

The individual's fatal relationship to nature is further complicated by the egotistical impulse to deny this kinship. In retrospect, Frankenstein knows that the winds will more likely yield a storm than calm, but in the blindness of his original optimism he believes that nature is hospitable to humanity, that it offers a Wordsworthian "ennobling interchange" that consoles and elevates the soul. Still trusting himself and the natural world, Frankenstein cries out with "something like joy" to the spirit of the Alps, as if it were a compassionate as well as a natural parent: "Wandering spirits . . . allow me this faint happiness, or take me, as your companion, away from the joys of life." But Frankenstein's belief in natural benevolence, like his earlier confidence in the benevolence of his desire, proves a trick of the wishful imagination. His request is answered by the true spirit of this and every place untamed by social conventions—the "superhuman," "unearthly" monster. Lulled once more by vanity and desire, Frankenstein recognizes the character of his bond with nature only when it again stands incarnate before him.

In order to understand why Mary Shelley's first readers did not fully appreciate what seems, in comparison to Romantic optimism, to be an unmistakable distrust of the imagination, we must turn to the monster's narrative. For Shelley's decision to divide the novel into a series of first-person narratives instead of employing a single perspective, whether first-person or omniscient, has the effect of qualifying her judgment of egotism. Because she dramatizes in the monster—not in Frankenstein—the psychological consequences of imaginative self-assertion, the reader is encouraged to participate not only in Frankenstein's desire for innate and natural benevolence but also in the agonizing repercussions of this misplaced optimism.

In the monster's narrative, Shelley both recapitulates Frankenstein's story and, ingeniously, completes it. Influenced by external circumstances that arouse, then direct, their desire for knowledge, both beings find that their imaginative quests yield only the terrible realization of an innate grotesqueness. But, unlike Frankenstein, the monster is denied the luxury of an original domestic harmony. The monster is "made," not born, and, as the product of the unnatural coupling of nature and the imagination, it is caught in the vortex of death that will ultimately characterize Frankenstein as well. Moreover, as the product, then the agent of Frankenstein's egotism, the monster is merely a link in the symbolic "series" of Frankenstein's "self-devoted being," not an autonomous member of a natural, organic family. Given a human's nobler aspirations without the accompanying power, the monster struggles futilely to deny both its status as a function of Frankenstein and the starkness of its circumscribed domain; the creature yearns to experience and act upon its own desires and to break free into the realistic frame that Frankenstein occupies. But the monster cannot have independent desires or influence its own destiny because, as the projection of Frankenstein's indulged desire and nature's essence, the creature *is* destiny. Moreover, because the monster's physical form literally embodies its essence, it cannot pretend to be something it is not; it cannot enter the human community it longs to join, and it cannot earn the sympathy it can all too vividly imagine. Paradoxically, the monster is the victim of both the symbolic and the literal. And, as such, it is doubly like a woman in patriarchal society—forced to be a symbol of (and vehicle for) someone else's desire, yet exposed (and exiled) as the deadly essence of passion itself.

For the monster, then, self-consciousness comes with brutal speed, for it depends, not on an act of transgression, but on literal self-perception. An old man's terror, a pool of water, a child's fear, all are nature's mirrors, returning the monster repeatedly to its grotesque self, "a figure hideously deformed and loathsome . . . a monster, a blot upon the earth." When the creature discovers its true origin—not in the literary works it finds and learns to read but in the records of Frankenstein's private experiments—it can no longer deny the absolute "horror" of its being, the monstrous singularity of egotism: "the minutest description of my odious and loathsome person is given, in language which painted your own horrors, and rendered mine ineffaceable." From this moment on, the monster's attempts to deny its nature are as futile as they are desperate. In its most elaborate scheme, the creature hides in a womblike hovel, as if it could be born again into culture by aping the motions of the family it spies upon. Although the monster tries to disguise its true nature by confronting only the blind old father, De Lacey's children return and recognize the creature's "ineffaceable" monstrosity for what it literally is. Their violent reaction, which the monster interprets as rejection by its "adopted family," at last precipitates the creature's innate nature; abandoning humanity's "godlike science"—the language of society it so diligently learned—for its natural tongue—the nonsignifying "fearful howlings" of beasts— the monster embarks on its systematic destruction of domestic harmony. The creature makes one final attempt to form a new society; but when Frankenstein refuses to create a female monster, it is condemned, like its maker, to a single bond of hatred. After Frankenstein's death, the monster disappears into the darkness at the novel's end, vowing to build its own funeral pyre; for it is as immune to human justice as it was repulsive to human love.

The monster carries with it the guilt and alienation that attend Frankenstein's self-assertion; yet, because Shelley realistically details the stages by which the creature is driven to act out its symbolic nature from *its* point of view, the reader is compelled to identify with its anguish and frustration. This narrative strategy precisely reproduces Mary Shelley's profound ambivalence toward Frankenstein's creative act; for by separating self-assertion from its consequences, she is able to dramatize both her conventional judgment of the evils of egotism and her emotional engagement in the imaginative act. Indeed, the pathos of the monster's cry suggests that Shelley identified most strongly with the product (and the victim) of Frankenstein's transgression: the objectified imagination, helpless and alone.

Although in an important sense, objectifying Frankenstein's imagination in the symbolic form of the monster delimits the range of connotations the imagination can have (it eliminates, for example, the possibilities of transcendent power or beneficence), this narrative strategy allows Shelley to express her ambivalence toward the creative act because a symbol is able to accommodate different, even contradictory, meanings. It is important to recognize that Shelley is using symbolism in a quite specific way here, a way that differs markedly from Percy Shelley's description of symbolism in his preface to the 1818 *Frankenstein*. In his justification for the central scene, Percy stresses not the ambivalence of the symbol but its comprehensiveness: "However impossible as a physical fact, [this incident] affords a point of view to the imagination for the delineating of human passions more comprehensive and commanding than any which the ordinary relations of existing events can yield." Although we know from the Shelley's letters and from the surviving manuscript of *Frankenstein* that Percy was instrumental in promoting and even revising the text, Mary did not uncritically or wholeheartedly accept the aesthetic program of which this self-confident use of symbolism was only one part. Instead, she transforms Percy's version of the Romantic aesthetic in such a way as to create for herself a nonassertive, and hence, acceptable, voice.

Percy Shelley defended his aesthetic doctrines, as part of his political and religious beliefs, with a conviction Mary later called a "resolution firm to martyrdom." Scornful of public opinion, he maintained that a true poet may be judged only by his legitimate peers, a jury "impaneled by Time from the selectest of the wise of many generations." Society's accusation that an artist is "immoral," he explains in the *Defence of Poetry* (1821), rests on "a misconception of the manner in which poetry acts to produce the moral improvement of man." The audience's relationship to poetry is based not on reason but on the imagination; true poetry does not encourage imitation or judgment but participation. It strengthens the individual's moral sense because it exercises and enlarges the capacity for sympathetic identification, that is, for establishing relationships. Following Plato, Percy declares that the primary reflex of the moral imagination is the outgoing gesture of love.

> The great secret of morals is Love; or a going out of our own nature, and an identification of ourselves with the beautiful which exists in thought, action, or person, not our own. A man, to be greatly good, must imagine intensely and comprehensively; he must put himself in the place of another and of many others; the pains and pleasures of his species must become his own. The great instrument of moral good is the imagination; and poetry administers to the effect by acting upon the cause.

Each of Percy Shelley's aesthetic doctrines comes to rest on this model of the imagination as an innately moral, capacious faculty. Because the imagination, if unrestrained, naturally supersedes relative morals (and in so doing compensates for the inhumaneness of the natural world), the poet should not discipline his or her poetic efforts according to a particular society's conceptions of right and wrong. Because the imagination tends to extend itself, through sympathy, to truth, the poet should simply depict examples of truth, thus drawing the audience into a relationship that simultaneously feeds and stimulates humanity's appetite for "thoughts of ever new delight."

This model of the artwork as an arena for relationships is the only aspect of Percy's aesthetics that Mary Shelley adopts without reservation. It seems to have been particularly appealing to her not only because it conforms to Percy's ideal but also because it satisfies society's conventional definition of proper feminine identity and proper feminine self-assertion. In doing so, it also answered needs and assuaged fears that seem to have been very pressing for Mary Shelley. As we have seen, she did not agree with Percy that the imagination is inherently moral. By the same token, she seems to have doubted that the abstract controls that Wollstonecraft described in her two *Vindications* and her *Letters Written . . . in Sweden* were capable of governing an individual's desire or disciplining the imagination. The factors that reinforced Shelley's doubt were probably as complicated as the anxieties themselves, but we can surmise that Percy Shelley's outspoken atheism helped undermine Mary's confidence in orthodox religion, that society's denigration of women's reasoning ability weakened her trust in that faculty, and that society's judgment and her own conflicting emotions conspired to make her doubt the morality of female feeling. For Mary Shelley, then, the only acceptable or safe arena in which to articulate her feelings, exercise her reason, and act out her unladylike ambition was that of personal relationships. In addition to the aesthetic purpose it serves, the narrative strategy of *Frankenstein* also provides just such a network of relationships. Because of its three-part narrative arrangement, Shelley's readers are drawn into a relationship with even the most monstrous part of the young author; Shelley is able to create her artistic persona through a series of relationships rather than a single act of self-assertion; and she is freed from having to take a single, definitive position on her unladylike subject. In other words, the narrative strategy of *Frankenstein*, like the symbolic presentation of the monster, enables Shelley to express and efface herself at the same time and thus, at least partially, to satisfy her conflicting desires for self-assertion and social acceptance.

Before turning to the 1831 revisions, we need to examine the last of the three narrators of *Frankenstein*; for if the scientist and the monster lure the reader ever deeper into the heart of ambition, Robert Walton, the mariner, reminds us that Frankenstein's abortive enthusiasm is *not* the only possible product of human energy. Walton's epistolary journal literally contains and effectively mediates the voices of the other two narrators, and so he may be said to have the last—if not the definitive—word. Like Henry Clerval and Felix De Lacey, Walton provides an example of the domesticated male, the alternative to Frankenstein's antisocial ambition. But because Walton bears closer affinities to his adopted friend than either Clerval or De Lacey does, his ability to deny his selfish desire and to replace it by concern for others stands as Shelley's most explicit criticism of Frankenstein's imaginative self-indulgence.

Like Frankenstein, Robert Walton is from his youth motivated by an imaginative obsession that scorns a literal-minded, superficial conception of nature. Despite known facts to the contrary, he believes that the North Pole is a "region of beauty and delight," and he longs to "satiate [his] ardent curiosity" by penetrating its secrets. Like Frankenstein's, Walton's ambition masquerades as a benevolent desire to benefit society, although it too is really only the egotist's desire for "glory." In his experiments, Frankenstein transgresses metaphysical boundaries; in his exploration, Walton defies geographical limitations; but for both, indulging desire is actually a transgression against domestic relationships. Walton's only living relative is Margaret Saville, the sister with whom his letters initially connect him; but as his ship sails farther into the icy wastes, his narrative becomes nearly as self-contained as Frankenstein's monologue, and the social gesture of writing letters gradually gives way to the more "self-devoted" habit of keeping a journal—a letter to his own future self.

Despite the similarities, however, Walton's ambition remains only an embryonic version of Frankenstein's murderous egotism, for ultimately he does not allow his obsession to destroy relationships. The crucial difference between them resides in Walton's willingness to deny his desire when it jeopardizes his social responsibilities or his relational identity. Walton constantly thinks of himself in terms of relationships: he is from his childhood an "affectionate brother," and he conceives of maturity as entailing extensions of this regulating influence. The "evil" he laments is not the mortality of the individual (as death was the "most irreparable evil" to Frankenstein) but the insufficiency that characterizes everyone.

> But I have one want which I have never yet been able to satisfy; and the absence of the object of which I now feel as a most severe evil. I have no friend, Margaret: when I am glowing with the enthusiasm of success, there will be none to

participate my joy. . . . I desire the company of a man who could sympathize with me; whose eyes would reply to mine. . . . My day dreams are . . . extended and magnificent; but they want (as the painters call it) *keeping*; and I greatly need a friend who would have sense enough not to despise me as romantic, and affection enough for me to endeavour to regulate my mind.

When his ship rescues the "wretched" Frankenstein from the frozen ocean, Walton immediately begins to "love him as a brother," to thaw his icy silence, to nurse him back to intermittent sympathy and generosity. But by this time Frankenstein's ambition has already shriveled his social passions into hatred and a craving for revenge ("I—I have lost every thing," he cries, "and cannot begin life anew." Only Walton is still capable of redirecting his involuted ambition outward into self-denying love, for he himself has never permitted his desire to escape completely from the regulating influence of social relationships. For example, in an early letter he claimed that his resolution was "as fixed as fate," but in that same letter he assured his sister that his concern for others would always override his ambition. And, in the end, of course, Walton capitulates to the pleas of his sailors—his family of the sea—and agrees to return south, to safety and civilization. Walton "kill[s] no albatross"; he realizes that denying his ambition will be painful, even humiliating, but he does not commit the antisocial crime of indulging his egotistic curiosity. Finally, his journal even opens outward again and addresses Margaret Saville directly. Walton's letters, as the dominant chain of all the narrations, preserve community despite Frankenstein's destructive self-devotion, for they link him and his correspondents (Mrs. Saville and the reader) in a relationship that Frankenstein can neither enter nor destroy.

THE 1831 REVISIONS

The revisions Mary Shelley prepared for the third edition of *Frankenstein*, which was published as part of Colburn and Bentley's Standard Novels Series in 1831, reveal that during the thirteen-year interval her interests had changed in two significant ways. The most extensive revisions, some of which were outlined soon after Percy's death in 1822, occur in chapters 1, 2, and 5 of Frankenstein's narrative; their primary effects are to idealize the domestic harmony of his childhood and to change the origin—and thus the implications—of his passionate ambition. As a consequence of the first alteration, Frankenstein's imaginative self-assertion becomes a more atrocious "crime"; as a result of the second, he is transformed from a realistic character to a symbol of the Romantic overreacher. Shelley's revisions thus extend her criticism of imaginative indulgence, already present in the 1818 text, and direct it much more pointedly at the blasphemy she now associates with her own adolescent audacity. Yet, paradoxically, even as she heightens the domestic destruction the egotist causes, she actually qualifies his responsibility. For in her new conception of Frankenstein's development she depicts him as the helpless pawn of a predetermined "destiny," a fate that is given, not made. The 1831 Frankenstein seems quintessentially a victim, like the monster, who now more precisely symbolizes what this kind of individual is rather than what he or she allows himself or herself to become. In both the text and her "Author's Introduction," Shelley suggests that such an individual has virtually no control over destiny and that, therefore, he or she is to be pitied rather than condemned.

The alteration almost all critics have noted is Shelley's reformulation of the relationship between Frankenstein and his fiancée Elizabeth. Originally a cousin, Elizabeth becomes a foundling in 1831—no doubt partly to avoid insinuations of incest—but also to emphasize the active benevolence of Frankenstein's mother, who, in adopting the poor orphan, is now elevated to the stature of a "guardian angel." This alteration, however, is only one of a series of changes that idealize the harmony of Frankenstein's childhood home. In this edition, for example, Shelley gives more space to the protectiveness of his parents and to the happiness of his childhood ("My mother's tender caresses, and my father's smile of benevolent pleasure while regarding me, are my first recollections"). Not surprisingly, Elizabeth, as the potential link between Frankenstein's childhood and his mature domesticity, receives the most attention. In 1831 she becomes much more like the Victorian Angel of the House; she is "a being heaven-sent," "a child fairer than pictured cherub." Elizabeth is both Frankenstein's guardian and his charge; explicitly, she embodies the regulating reciprocity of domestic love. "She was the living spirit of love to soften and attract: I might have become sullen in my study, rough through the ardour of my nature, but that she was there to subdue me to a semblance of her own gentleness." By emphasizing Elizabeth's pivotal role in what is now an ideal domestic harmony, Shelley prepares to heighten the devastating social consequences of Frankenstein's imaginative transgression and to further underscore the loss *he* suffers through his willful act.

Despite this idealization of the family, in the 1831 version the seeds of Frankenstein's egotism germinate more rapidly within the home, for Shelley now attributes his fall not primarily to accidents or to his departure but to his own innate "temperature" or character. "Deeply smitten with the thirst for knowledge," Frankenstein is now from his birth set apart from his childhood companions. Unlike the "saintly" Elizabeth or the "noble spirit[ed]" Clerval, Frankenstein has a violent temper and vehement passions. His accidental discovery of Agrippa is now preceded by a description of a more decisive factor, the determining "law in [his] temperature"; it is this innate predilection that turns his imagination "not toward childish pursuits, but to an eager desire to learn . . . the secrets of heaven and earth." In 1831 Shelley retains Frankenstein's suggestion that his father's negligence contributed to his "fatal impulse," but almost every alteration contradicts the implication that circumstances can substantially alter innate character. In 1831 Frankenstein resists modern science not because "some accident" prevents him from attending lectures but because "one of those caprices of the mind" distracts him from scientific speculations. By further emphasizing the moralists' description of the imagination's irrepressible energy, Shelley radically reduces the importance of external circumstances and underscores the inevitability of the overreacher's fall. At the same time, she also pushes what had been a realistic narrative, framing the symbolic story of monstrous egotism, in the direction of allegory.

Shelley graphically dramatizes the "fatality" of Frankenstein's character in terms of a contest.

> Thus strangely are our souls constructed, and by such slight ligaments are we bound to prosperity or ruin. When I look back, it seems to me as if this almost miraculous change of inclination and will was the immediate suggestion of the guardian angel of my life—the last effort made by the spirit of preservation to avert the storm that was even then hanging in the stars, and ready to envelope me. . . . It was a strong effort of the spirit of good; but it was ineffectual. Destiny was too potent, and her immutable laws had decreed my utter and terrible destruction.

Characterizing Frankenstein's psyche as a battleground between the personified "spirit of good" and "destiny" blurs the distinction between personal ambition and external coercion and gives the impression that, in an important sense, Frankenstein is merely the passive victim of powerful forces. This impression is reinforced by other crucial alterations in the 1831 text. When Frankenstein sets out for Ingolstadt, for example, he characterizes himself as being hostage to an irresistible "influence," to which he attributes a relentless intentionality: "Chance—or rather the evil influence, the Angel of Destruction . . . asserted omnipotent sway over me from the moment I turned my reluctant steps from my father's door." This "influence" has its counterpart in Frankenstein's own ambition, but, once more, Shelley personifies its workings so as to make Frankenstein seem a victim:

> Such were the professor's words—rather let me say such the words of fate, enounced to destroy me. As he [M. Waldman] went on, I felt as if my soul were grappling with a palpable enemy; one by one the various keys were touched which formed the mechanism of my being: chord after chord was sounded, and soon my mind was filled with one thought, one conception, one purpose. So much has been done, exclaimed the soul of Frankenstein,—more, far more, will I achieve. . . . I closed not my eyes that night. My internal being was in a state of insurrection and turmoil; I felt that order would thence arise, but I had no power to produce it.

This remarkable passage suggests that one's "soul" can be taken over by an invading enemy, who, having taken up residence within, effectively becomes one's "fate." The "palpable enemy," which we know to be imaginative desire, is no stranger to its chosen victim; but Shelley's repeated use of the passive voice and her depiction of the "soul" as a vessel to be filled, then objectified, makes this "resolution" seem a visitation rather than an act of self-indulgence. Dramatizing the fragmentation of Frankenstein's psyche foreshadows, of course, the literal splitting-off of the monster; but, equally important, it suggests that Frankenstein cannot be held responsible for the "destiny" he is powerless to resist.

In 1831 Shelley also elaborates Frankenstein's misunderstanding of the natural world; but by extending his blindness to the most innocent of all the characters, Elizabeth, Shelley now makes him seem only one victim of nature's treachery. In the revised version of the scene in the Alps, Frankenstein's deception is all the more cruel because nature now specifically invokes memories of his harmonious childhood and even presents the face of his deceased mother: "The very winds whispered in soothing accents, and maternal nature bade me weep no more. . . . The same lulling sounds acted as a lullaby to my too keen sensations. . . . [The forms of nature] gathered around me, and bade me be at peace." But this nature still holds only the monster; and when Frankenstein's trust and betrayal are generalized to Elizabeth, his delusion becomes an inevitable curse of the human condition, not simply a production of his own unleashed imagination. In her revised letter in chapter 6, Elizabeth celebrates nature's benevolent constancy: "The blue lake, and snow-clad mountains, they never change;—and I think our placid home, and our contented hearts are regulated by the same immutable laws." But when Justine is executed, Elizabeth also learns the bitter truth. In this context, her heart-rending speech ("misery has come home, and men appear to me as monsters"), retained from the 1818 text, now emphasizes less that Elizabeth is Frankenstein's victim than that all humans are unwitting victims of nature's violence and their own natural frailty.

As one might expect, in 1831 Shelley also alters her portrait of Robert Walton in order to remove the alternative of self-control she now wants to deny to Frankenstein. Walton's victory over egotism becomes less a triumph over his own ambition than the consequence of a mysterious internal revolution. Initially Walton describes himself as a man driven by two conflicting tendencies:

> There is something at work in my soul, which I do not understand. I am practically industrious—pains-taking;—a workman to execute with perseverence and labour:—but besides this, there is a love for the marvellous, a belief in the marvellous, intertwined in all my projects, which hurries me out of the common pathways of men, even to the wild sea and unvisited regions I am about to explore.

Walton too is a pawn of internal forces, forces which seem to originate from outside him ("there is a love . . . which hurries me"). Thus, although in 1831 Walton's ambition is more pronounced, more like the young Frankenstein's, he is not wholly responsible for his actions. Just as M. Waldman was the external catalyst to precipitate Frankenstein's "destiny," so Frankenstein serves as the critical agent for Walton. Frankenstein's narrative resolves Walton's internal conflict and restores to him the domestic affection that has all along formed the innate "groundwork of [his] character." Walton does not really assert himself or actively choose; rather, true to his character, his original self-denying nature, he allows himself to be acted on by others: to respond to the needs of Frankenstein, then to the sailors in his charge.

Of the three narrations that compose *Frankenstein*, the monster's history receives the least attention in the 1831 revisions—no doubt because Mary Shelley sympathized even more strongly with the guilt and alienation that shadow the egotist's crime. Moreover, by implication, the monster is now the appropriate extension of the curse of the creative artist, not the product of the self-indulged imagination. The monster's grotesqueness and its singularity are still signs of an essential transgression, but its pathetic powerlessness is now a more appropriate counterpart to the helplessness of Frankenstein himself.

We can begin to understand the significance these charges held for Mary Shelley by examining the introduction she added to the 1831 text. Her primary desire in this introduction is to explain—and justify—the audacity of what now seems to her like blasphemy; she wants to answer, and thus forever silence, the question that, repeatedly asked, insistently raises the ghost of her former self: "How I, then a young girl, came to think of, and to dilate upon, so very hideous an idea?" Even *this* explanation must be justified, however, for Mary Shelley wants most of all to assure her readers that she is no longer the defiant, self-assertive "girl" who once dared to explore ambition and even to seek fame herself without the humility proper to a lady. Now "infinitely indifferent" to literary reputation, Shelley claims to be "very averse to bringing [her]self forward in print." Her commentary is permissible only because she introduces it as coming from and explaining her author-persona, that other self, which is, strictly speaking, not the "personal" Mary Shelley at all: "as it will be confined to such topics as have connection with my authorship alone, I can scarcely accuse myself of a personal intrusion." This splitting of herself into two personae replicates Shelley's narrative strategy of apportioning her sympathies among the various characters in the novel. Just as she did—and did not—identify with the monster, so she is—and is not—responsible for giving substance to her dream.

Her 1831 version of the dream that inspired the novel makes clear what Shelley is so eager to disavow: the monster's creator, now referred to specifically as an artist, transgresses the bounds of propriety through his art. This trangression (now characterized as blasphemy) is followed by the artist's fear and revulsion, for he recognizes in his "odious handywork" the essential meaning of artistic creation: the "yellow, watery, but speculative eyes" that mirror the artist's own are the signs not only of transgression but of a fundamental deficiency common to creature and creator alike.

> I saw the pale student of unhallowed arts kneeling beside the thing he had put together. I saw the hideous phantasm of a man stretched out, and then, on the working of some powerful engine, show signs of life, and stir with an uneasy, half vital motion. Frightful must it be; for supremely frightful would be the effect of any human endeavour to mock the stupendous mechanism of the Creator of the world. His success would terrify the artist; he would rush away from his odious handywork, horror-stricken. He would hope that, left to itself, the slight spark of life which he had communicated would fade; that this thing, which had received such imperfect animation, would subside into dead matter; and he might sleep in the belief that the silence of the grave would quench for ever the transient existence of the hideous corpse which he had looked upon as the cradle of life. He sleeps; but he is awakened; he opens his eyes; behold the horrid thing stands at his bedside, opening his curtains, and looking on him with yellow, watery, but speculative eyes.

The boldness with which Shelley once pursued metaphysical speculations now seems, first of all, a defiance of one's proper place—here the male's in relation to God, but also, by extension, woman's in relation to the family. Clearly here, as in the thematic emphasis of the novel, Shelley expresses the tension she feels between the self-denial demanded by domestic activity and the self-assertiveness essential to artistic creation. Before 1816, she explains, she did not respond to Percy's encouragement that she write because "travelling, and the cares of a family, occupied [her] time." Now that she has pursued his designs, she finds literary production to be a perverse substitute for a woman's natural function: a "hideous corpse" usurps what should be the "cradle of life."

But the "speculative" monster is also an objectification of the artist's creative self, and as such it raises disturbing associations for the real Mary Shelley. Because this society tends to objectify women in cultural forms ranging from symbols of property to poetic muses, the temptation to think of oneself as an object constitutes a particularly seductive danger for women. Certainly Mary Shelley's personal testimony proves that self-objectification was both an alluring and a terrifying temptation for her for some very specific reasons. In her culture, objects and nature and women and the literal, as versions of the Other in opposition to which the Subject seeks definition, are all on the same side of the conceptual axis. And for Shelley, as we have seen, the common denominator of all of these is death. Objectification for Shelley therefore means not only conforming to the masculine stereotype of women but, more ominously, exiling herself into the object world of nature—ironically, "maternal nature"—which harbors both the murderous egotism Shelley feared in herself and the deadly blight of the literal. As Mary Shelley imagines her female self, she gives her own conflicted energy the form of a monster, a vivified corpse that is capable of commanding pity but that, in all its actions and despite its intentions, destroys every living being it touches. And as she imagines the act of creativity, she imagines exiling her own imaginative energy into a landscape that is fatal to figuration and that freezes all attempts to transform or disguise the self. In such a world, the monster—and, by extension, the female artist—is doomed; in the object world of nature, even one who longs to speak and who acquires eloquence from the tablescraps of patriarchal culture, finds that language loses its power to create more than curiosity or revulsion.

As this description suggests, however, the terror that Shelley associates with artistic creation comes not just from the guilt of exceeding one's proper role or from the fatal claims of the literal; it comes also from the fear of failure that accompanies such presumption. The creation Shelley imagines is "odious," "horrid," "hideous," imperfectly animated—a failure for all to see. Earlier in the 1831 introduction she had also suggested that the anxiety generated by artistic creation emanates in large part from its profoundly public nature. There she distinguished between her youthful, private fantasies of pure imagination ("waking dreams . . . which had for their subject the formation of a succession of imaginary incidents") and the stories she actually wrote down, the "close imitations" she shared with her childhood friend, Isabel Baxter. "My dreams were at once more fantastic and agreeable than my writings," she explains. "The airy flights of . . . imagination," in fact, she considers her only "true compositions," for what she wrote was in "a most common-place style." Whereas Mary Wollstonecraft, in *The Rights of Woman* at least, conceived of writing as confrontation with authorities, for Shelley, to write is necessarily to imitate, and her models, almost all masculine, are both intimidating and potentially judgmental of her audacious foray into their domain. Thus Shelley automatically anticipates their censure of what seems even to her to be the monstrous inadequacy of her objectified self. The fear of public scrutiny and judgment lies behind most of Shelley's disclaimers of the artistic enterprise: "What I wrote was intended at least for one other eye—my childhood's companion and friend; but my dreams were all my own; I accounted for them to nobody; they were my refuge when annoyed—my dearest pleasure when free." For Mary Shelley, when the imagination is placed in the service of a text, a discomforting transformation occurs: what had been a harmless pastime becomes tantamount to a transgression, and, fueling the attendant guilt, the fear surfaces that if she does compete she will be found inadequate. Only the unbound and therefore nonbinding imagination can escape censure and thus protect the dreamer against exposure and pain.

Shelley's distinction between imagination and imaginative creation would have surprised many of her male contemporaries. In his *Defence of Poetry*, for example, Percy Shelley does not even consider the possibility of keeping imaginative insights private, for, in his theory, poets have a profoundly public responsibility; they are the "unacknowledged legislators of the world." Percy's description centers on the self-expressive function of art; he derives his authority from a masculine tradition of poet-prophets and his self-confidence from the social approval generally accorded to masculine self-assertion. Lacking the support of both tradition and public opinion, however, and lacking her mother's determination, Mary Shelley separates the permissible, even liberating expression of the imagination from the more egotistical, less defensible act of public self-assertion. For Mary Shelley, the imagination is properly a vehicle for escaping the self, not a medium of personal power or even self-expression. She therefore associates the imagination with images of flight, escape, and freedom; writing she associates with monstrosity, transgression, and failure. If her male peers would have found this distinction incomprehensible, her mother would have understood it all too well; for Shelley's ideal "art" is very like the "feminine" artistry that Wollstonecraft criticized in *Maria*: it not only lacks "substance," but it is completely ineffectual as well.

Mary Shelley did not, of course, wholly reject the artistic enterprise, no matter how genuine her anxieties and no matter how abject her apologies. . . . By 1831 Shelley was an established professional author; she was supporting herself and her son almost exclusively by writing; and her numerous reviews and stories, as well as her three novels, had earned her a considerable reputation. Nor does she totally disavow kinship with her younger self, the more defiant Mary Godwin. It is with felt intensity that Shelley vividly recalls her feeling of power when, having dared to imagine a "frightful . . . success," the younger Mary triumphantly silenced her male critics: "Swift as light and as cheering was the idea that broke in upon me. 'I have found it!' . . . On the morrow I announced that I had *thought of a story.*" But in 1831, the mature Mary Shelley is able to countenance the creation of *Frankenstein*—and, in effect, the creation of her entire artistic role— only because she can interpret these creations as primarily the work of other people and of external circumstances. Thus Shelley "remembers" (sometimes inaccurately) the origin of *Frankenstein* in such a way as to displace most of the responsibility for what might otherwise seem willful self-assertion; essentially she offers a story that depicts the young Mary Godwin as a creation of others, a pawn, like Frankenstein, of forces larger than herself. Twice she insists on Percy's role in her project, his repeated desire that she "prove [herself] worthy of [her] parentage, and enrol [herself] on the page of fame": "He was for ever inciting me to obtain literary reputation," she adds. She also (incorrectly) recalls the pressure her companions at Diodati exerted on her to produce a ghost story for their contest. The degree of embarrassment she records and the vividness of this inaccurate recollection suggest both the extent to which she internalized the expectations she assumed her companions would have and how important it was that the impetus for her creativity should come from outside. "*Have you thought of a story?* I was asked each morning, and each morning I was forced to reply with a mortifying negative." To protect herself, however, Shelley assures herself and the reader that she never entered directly into competition with her intimidating male companions. "The illustrious poets," Byron and Percy Shelley, soon tired of the "platitude of prose," and "poor Polidori" is hardly worth considering (perhaps because both poets openly ridiculed the doctor). "The machinery of a story" is the humblest of all inventions, she continues, diminishing her accomplishment to what she now considers its appropriate stature. All invention, in fact, she reduces to mere piecework: "invention, it must be humbly admitted . . . can give form to dark, shapeless substances, but it cannot bring into being the substance itself." Even the "substance" of her story, she is quick to add, comes from external sources: initially, her dream was inspired by a conversation between Byron and Percy, "to which [Mary] was a devout but nearly silent listener."

Finally, Shelley dramatizes her own contribution to these ideas ("moulding and fashioning") as if it were nearly involuntary:

> When I placed my head on my pillow, I did not sleep, nor could I be said to think. My imagination, unbidden, possessed and guided me, gifting the successive images that arose in my mind with a vividness far beyond the usual bounds of reverie. I saw—with shut eyes, but acute mental vision,—I saw the pale student of unhallowed arts kneeling before the thing he had put together.

Then follows the text of the dream quoted above.

The waking vision "possesses" Shelley, just as the fateful, "palpable enemy" possessed the 1831 Frankenstein. "Horror-stricken" like her imagined artist, Shelley tries to "exchange the ghastly image of [her] fancy for the realities around"—"the dark *parquet*, the closed shutters" of her room. But she finds that she cannot escape the "hideous phantom" except by "transcribing" her "waking dream." In other words, she can exorcise the specter of her own egotistical imagination only by giving in to it as if to a foreign power—no matter how guardedly, with no matter what guilt.

In 1831, then, when Shelley revised her depiction of Frankenstein, she invested him with both the guilt she had come to associate with her original audacity and the feeling of helplessness she had learned to invoke in order to sanction and explain that audacity. In her need to justify her metaphysical boldness, she employs an almost Godwinian notion of Necessity: Frankenstein's "character" is Fate incarnate; the artist, driven by Necessity, shadowed by guilt, is the powerless midwife to the birth of such "fatality" within human society itself. Paradoxically, this wholehearted acceptance of an essentially subordinate and passive role—like the symbolic presentation of the monster—affords Mary Shelley precisely the grounds she needed to sanction her artistic career. For the claim to powerlessness provides a socially acceptable rationale for self-aggrandizement and thus a means of satisfying, simultaneously, her need for social approval and her desire to "prove [herself] worthy" of her parents and Percy Shelley. In her depictions of the monster and the 1831 Frankenstein, Mary Shelley elevates feminine helplessness to the stature of myth. The elaboration of that myth—and her own place within it—proves to be the task of the remainder of Shelley's literary career. As a young girl she discovered both the monstrosity and the price of her own ambitions; as a grown woman she experienced a persistent desire to disguise that aggression beneath the manners of the proper lady her society promised that every girl could grow up to be.

The Negative Oedipus: Father, *Frankenstein*, and the Shelleys

William Veeder

> It was Grandfather's and when Father gave it to me he said, Quentin, I
> give you the mausoleum of all hope and desire. . . . I give it to you not
> that you may remember time, but that you might forget it now and then for a
> moment and not spend all your breath trying to conquer it.
>
> Quentin Compson, in FAULKNER, *The Sound and the Fury*

> A son can never, in the fullest sense, become a father. Some amount of
> amateur effort is possible. A son may after honest endeavor produce what
> some people might call, technically, children. But he remains a son. In the
> fullest sense.
>
> DONALD BARTHELME, *The Dead Father*

Defining the role of father in Mary Shelley has been both fostered and
impeded by recent criticism. Feminist theory with its recognition of
the importance of *mother* has prevented any overrating of father. In the
context of Kleinian arguments by Nancy Chodorow and Dorothy
Dinnerstein that Freud's neglect of the pre-oedipal years caused him
to seriously undervalue the maternal role in child development, literary
critics such as Sandra Gilbert and Susan Gubar, Mary Jacobus, Mary
Poovey, Marc A. Rubenstein, and Janet M. Todd have established
convincingly the importance of Mary Wollstonecraft for Mary Shelley.
Feminist readings can, however, go too far in this direction. Mother
can achieve such prominence that father is cast into shadow. Poovey's
chapters are the best overall appraisal of Mary Shelley's novelistic
carrier that I know, but I cannot agree that "in Mary Shelley's own
youth and in *Falkner* (and, in a slightly different sense, in *Frankenstein*)

From *Critical Inquiry* 12, no. 2 (Winter 1986). © 1986 by the University of Chicago.

the motherless daughter's relationship with the father carries the burden of needs originally and ideally satisfied by the mother; in a sense, the relationship with each father is only an imaginative substitute for the absent relationship with the mother." Mary Shelley in fact insisted upon the superiority of a father's tuition for daughters, devoted much of her fiction to father-directed emotions and events, confessed privately to untoward affection for Godwin, and expressed this affection so shockingly in *Mathilda* that her father suppressed the novel.

A second approach to Mary Shelley, that of the psychoanalytic critics of *Frankenstein*, does give prominence to father, since the oedipal model presupposes generational conflict. Preeminence, however, is once again accorded to mother. The primary object of Frankenstein's affection is presumed to be his mother Caroline, and the primary object of his scientific labors is presumed to be the discovery of a principle of life which would bring her back from the dead. Despite unquestionably valuable insights by J. M. Hill, Gordon D. Hirsch, Morton Kaplan and Robert Kloss, Rubenstein, U. C. Knoepflmacher, and others, the oedipal model has tended to occlude deeper levels of the psyche were Mary Shelley moves beyond mother love. Here Freud's "negative" Oedipus provides a more useful paradigm, because here the son desires to murder *mother* in order to get to *father*.

My study of Mary Shelley and father includes her husband because Percy Shelley's obsessions with patriarchy, with " 'GOD, AND KING, AND LAW,' " influenced profoundly Mary's art and life. Percy's idealizations of father in *The Revolt of Islam* and *Prince Athanase* indicated ways of resolving familial antagonisms which Mary adopted and developed in her later fiction. Percy's relationship with *Frankenstein* is still more intricate. Recognizing that her husband's obsessions with father and self-creation were contributing to the deterioration of their marriage, Mary represents these obsessions (among many others, including her own) in Victor Frankenstein—partly to vent in art the anger which would have further damaged the marriage, and partly to show Percy before it was too late the errors of his ways. It was too late. Percy responded to *Frankenstein* in *Prometheus Unbound* and *The Cenci* with a reaffirmation of sonship which has been largely unrecognized by scholars.

Father looms so large for both Mary and Percy Shelley that no one critical approach can account for him fully. At their most idealistic—and thus most traditional—the Shelleys encourage a critical methodology which integrates the traditional disciplines of biographical and close textual analyses. By taking this approach to Mary's later fiction and to

Percy's *The Revolt of Islam*, I can not only confirm the prominence of father for the Shelleys but also establish the ideal against which their most subversive and important art was created. Reading this indirect, overdetermined art in light of the negative Oedipus will help answer important questions about *Frankenstein, Prometheus Unbound,* and *The Cenci* and will, I hope, add to our understanding of the vexed role of father in the Romantic period and in subsequent generations whose children we are.

I. The Ideal

In a biographical nexus as amazing as the persons involved, Percy's intricate conflicts with father are illuminated by Mary's incestuous attractions to father. Mary's admiration for Mary Wollstonecraft, unquestionable though it is, cannot match the intensity of what she called "my excessive and romantic attachment to my Father." Mary, like her Mathilda, "clung to the memory of my parents; my mother I should never see, she was dead: but the idea of [my] unhappy, wandering father was the idol of my imagination." The primacy of father is confirmed by Mathilda's knowledgeable steward: " 'You are like her [your mother] although there is more of my lord in you.' " Although she reveres Mary Wollstonecraft as a theorist of pedagogy, Mary Shelley insists upon the advantages of a father's tuition. "There is a peculiarity in the education of a daughter, brought up by a father only, which tends to develop early a thousand of those portions of mind, which are folded up, and often destroyed, under mere feminine tuition" [*Lodore*]. In her last novels Mary continues to insist how much fathers love daughters. *Perkin Warbeck* features the heroic mariner De Faro who "could not prevail on himself to leave his lovely, unprotected girl behind"; *Falkner* attests that "no father ever worshipped a child so fervently" as the title character does his Elizabeth. Mary never gets over Godwin's coldness. She is forty-one years old when she says "My Father, from age and domestic circumstances, could not '*me faire valoir*.' " Even in middle age, Mary can bring herself to this terrible admission only by insulating the reality in French phrasing (when English would suffice), in italics (which she does not always apply to foreign expressions), in quotation marks (which are unnecessary), and by atoning for the aggression by capitalizing "My Father" (which she by no means always does).

Percy too makes father paramount. The intensity of his feelings—

which finds negative expression in *The Mask of Anarchy*'s rage at
" 'GOD, AND KING, AND LAW' " and at his father, Sir Timothy—
expresses itself positively in Percy's lifelong search for lawgivers. After
Dr. James Lind, who taught science, occult lore, and the right to be
different, comes Thomas Jefferson Hogg. "I [Percy] took you for one
who was to give laws to us poor beings who grovel beneath." Then
Percy finds Godwin. The older man's enormous authority comes in
part from his confirming what the young philosopher needs to believe—
that reason can control passion and assure perfection. But Godwin also
answers the needs of a rebellious son. Jean Overton Fuller has it
backward when she says that "from the time he [Shelley] read this
[*Political Justice*], he regarded the circumstances of his birth as shaming,
and only possible to live down by the dedication of his mind and
position to the elevation of those less endowed." Percy's rebelliousness
predates his reading of *Political Justice* because his anger was father-
directed before it was political. Godwin thus serves less to generate
rebellion than to legitimize it. He lessens the guilt while encouraging
the crime. Godwin allows the son both to have *him* as new father and
to have a nonpsychological and thus largely guiltless rationale for
rejecting the old father.

Mary can see so accurately into Percy because she shares with him
more than an obsession with father: daughter and son here desire the
same man, William Godwin.

Percy and Mary both project their desires for father onto the
screen of art. Seeing how desire is satisfied ideally there will help us to
understand both why such satisfactions prove impossible in the Shelley's marriage and how their dissatisfactions are figured forth in
Frankenstein. A convenient starting point is the passage in Percy's *Revolt
of Islam* where Laon sees Cnthna's corpse hanging from a tree:

> A woman's shape, now lank and cold and blue,
>   The dwelling of the many-coloured worm,
> Hung there; the white and hollow creek I drew
>   To my dry lips . . .
>
> .   .   .   .
>   —in the deep
> The shape of an old man did then appear,
> Stately and beautiful; that dreadful sleep
> His heavenly smiles dispersed, and I could wake and weep.
>   (*The Revolt of Islam*, ll. 1333–36, 1347–50)

Union with the father can occur in *The Revolt of Islam* only after woman is removed. Kissing hanged Cythna's "hollow cheek" (l. 1335) cannot relieve Laon's physical and spiritual dessication, but the Hermit as good father is androgynous enough to be female as well as male. His "solemn" voice is "sweet"; his "giant" arms nurse Laon tenderly (ll. 1357, 1364). First the physical dessication is relieved ("my scorched limbs he wound, / In linen moist and balmy" [ll. 1365–66]), then the spiritual. "That aged man, so grand and mild, / Tended me, even as some sick mother seems / To hang in hope over a dying child" (ll. 1401–3). Since the Hermit is equally effectual in the manly arts—he controls the intellectual discussion as decisively as he "ruled the helm" of the ship—he could prove overbearing (l. 1380). In fact, Laon initially feared "it was a fiend" (l. 1383). But the Hermit does not play the heavy father. Like his model Dr. Lind who defended Percy against Sir Timothy, the Hermit can cut the Old Ones down to size with "a glance as keen as is the lightning's stroke / When it doth rive the knots of some ancestral oak" (ll. 1466–67).

Up to this point Percy has been following the precedent of Wordsworth's *Excursion*: Youth-in-need-of-Wisdom finds all-wise-aged-Man. But *The Excursion* fails, as Percy (in effect, if not consciously) sees it, to recognize that discipleship is only half the battle. No matter how devoted a pupil the son is, he can never achieve full manhood and thus can never get beyond the natural, inevitable emotions of aggression and alienation. *The Excursion* offered the son no way out because it confined him to a single-staged relationship with an elder who dispensed wisdom in propositional statements (" 'the good die first' ") and in exemplary tales ("The Ruined Cottage"). Thus the best the younger man could do was to acknowledge and embrace the elder's wisdom.

From such permanent dependence Percy finds an escape by insisting that the father-son relationship be two-staged. Although his Hermit does address Laon's problems, Percy presents no propositional statements and no exemplary tales. In fact he allows the Hermit no dialogue at all at this point in *Islam*. The elder's role here is largely maternal: he creates a nurturing ambience in which the young man's psyche heals itself. Then stage two can begin. The son takes over the role of Wordsworth's seer and provides the elder with ideas and the "power" to effect them.

> I have been thy passive instrument
>
> .   .   .   .
>
> thou has lent
> To me, to all, the power to advance
> Towards unforeseen deliverance.
>
> (ll. 1549, 1551–53)

Likening Laon's tongue to "a lance" (l. 1566), the Hermit confirms the son's phallic manhood by crediting him with that transition from language to action which the father could never make.

Son also surpasses sire in *Prince Athanase* where the Wordsworth situation is again reversed:

> The youth, as shadows on a grassy hill
> Outrun the winds that chase them, soon outran
> His teacher, and did teach with native skill
>
> Strange truths and new to that experienced man;
> Still they were friends.
>
> (ll. 176–80)

This last line is crucial for *Islam* as well as for *Prince Athanase*. In surpassing the father, the son must not generate a guilt that would blight his flowering manhood. In the bloody battle against tyranny in *Islam*, Laon "in joy . . . found, / Beside me then, firm as a giant pine / Among the mountain-vapours driven around, / The old man whom I loved" (ll. 2416–19). The Hermit's progress from ruined tower (ll. 1415–16) to towering pine does not indicate any maturation on his part. The growth is Laon's. The phallic pine's association with father establishes that Laon is now confident enough of his own powers to recognize the manhood of his father and of every other male. A benign coda is now possible. The Hermit's glorious death in battle can complete the generational transfer because father and son have achieved the only equality possible to creatures bound upon the wheel of time. Each is assured the dignity of his place in the generational cycle.

The problem of Mary's "excessive and romantic attachment" to Godwin finds in her later fiction a resolution which is as idealized and conventional as Percy's in *Islam*.

> On a bed of [forest] leaves lay an old man [a Hermit]: his grey hairs were thinly strewn on his venerable temples, his beard white, flowing and soft, fell to his girdle; he smiled

even in his sleep a gentle smile of benevolence. I knelt down
beside him; methought it was my excellent father.

All her life Mary as well as Percy is the child in the fairy-tale who
wanders through the psychic forest seeking father. He materializes in
Valperga as he did in *Islam*, to fulfill through art the fantasy denied in
life. Like Percy's Hermit, Mary's is all-sufficient because androgynous.
"Soft . . . gentle . . . benevolence" signal his feminine capacity to
nurture, while the role of "father" as spiritual guide assures his masculine authority. "Venerable" characterizes this "excellent father" as it
did Percy's surrogate father in "The Coliseum"; a smile associated
with sleep establishes the benignity of both *Valperga*'s Hermit and
Islam's. The conjunction here of "temples" and "knelt" reflects the
willingness of both Shelleys to revere properly androgynous paternity.

The quest for father recurs in virtually all of Mary's novels.
Besides the patently incestuous *Mathilda* where the mother's death frees
daughter and father for untoward desires, there is *Falkner*, where the
mother's death impels Elizabeth toward a foster father; *Lodore*, where
the mother's abandonment of her daughter assures Ethel's dependence
upon "the only parent she had ever known"; *Perkin Warbeck*, where
motherless Monina returns to her manly father after intervals of (platonic) devotion to Perkin; and *Valperga*, where Euthanasia considers
her bond with father "the dearest tie she had to earth" and where
orphaned Beatrice venerates both "my excellent father" the Hermit
and "my good father, the bishop." The abundance of motherless
heroines in nineteenth-century fiction indicates the appeal of this situation to the culture: how much more strongly does it affect Mary
Godwin whose situation it actually is.

Fathers in Mary's later fiction satisfy ideally a daughter's need for
physical, psychological, and intellectual support, but there are also
more intensely charged emotions which must be defused. The repetition of "she idolized her father," "her idolized father," and "her father
whom she idolized" seems particularly obsessive because three different heroines are involved: Ethel in *Lodore*, Elizabeth in *Falkner*, Clara in
The Last Man. The obsession is Mary Godwin's. She insists, however,
that incestuous feelings are reciprocal. Whereas it is the daughter in
Falkner who "felt herself bound . . . by stronger than filial ties," the
father is the one who knows "more than a father's fondness" in *Lodore*.
Such fondness makes him the aggressor, "penetrating the depths of her
soul' with his "dark expressive eyes," while it is the "rapturous"

daughter in *Falkner* whose "thrilling adoration . . . dreamt not of the necessity of a check, and luxuriated in its boundless excess." When Elizabeth exclaims, " 'God preserve you, my more than father,' " Mary Godwin is speaking.

Feelings more than daughterly are frequent in nineteenth-century fiction, but incest is not. The traditional way to channel untoward emotion is followed by Mary Shelley in her fiction after *Mathilda*. Suitors replace sires. In a century when bridegrooms were admonished endlessly to carry on the parental guidance of the weaker vessel, Neville is told by Falkner " 'You must compensate to my dear child for my loss—you must be father as well as husband.' " Neville can replace Falkner so smoothly because he is in fact the same character. Similar physically (dark, olive, craggy) and psychologically (prone to macho rage but open to feminine influence), both men live under the same cloud, "the mysterious wretchedness that darkened the lives of the only two beings, the inner emotions of whose souls had been opened to her." Although Elizabeth encourages Neville in the quest for his mother's killer which eventually brings Falkner to trial, Elizabeth's endeavors are therapeutic, not punitive. Only after Falkner has publicly confessed his part in Alithea's death can he be forgiven by Neville and be reconciled to him. Only *then* can the triangle of Elizabeth–Neville–Falkner be assured permanence. The conventional marriage which resolves the love plot thus provides an unconventional wish fulfillment. *Falkner* ends not with the wedding of Ethel and Neville but with the cemented bond between Neville and Falkner because only the union of suitor and father assures that the daughter can at last consummate the passion which has driven Mary's heroines. And herself.

Why does Mary not find with Percy the resolution of complexes and the completeness of union which Ethel achieves with Neville? Mary certainly tries to put *Falkner* into practice—to move from father to suitor by recreating the elder man in the younger. "Until I met Shelley I [could?] justly say that he [Godwin] was my God." Mary abandons herself to Percy with the most orthodox completeness. "Perhaps [I] will one day have a father till then be every thing to me love." Mary of course remains deeply concerned with Godwin, but she makes Percy her god—investing "everything" in him and expecting as much in return. If she has gotten beyond father ties and united permanently with Percy, why can't he get beyond father problems and unite exclusively with her? *Islam* seems to second Mary's espousal of the "normal" teleology of relationships. After the Hermit's death, Cythna—who, it turns out, is not actually dead—reenters the plot and is united with Laon in ecstatic congress.

Why art and life don't reflect each other for Percy will become clearer if we turn back to *Islam* and see that beneath its apparently idealistic surface are subversive forces at work. Why does Percy put himself in the awkward position of having to resurrect Cythna? Why hang her in the first place? If Laon needs to be alone with the Hermit to achieve solidarity, Cythna's capture and abduction at this point in the plot are convenient enough. The very unnecessariness of Cythna's hanging indicates how necessary it must be to Percy. Especially since her corpse is presented so gruesomely, the assassination of woman—as opposed to her absence—seems a precondition of male solidarity for Percy.

Islam reverses *Falkner* by paralleling it too exactly. Percy as well as Mary is seeking father *as end*. The ostensibly similar teleologies of daughter going beyond father to suitor and son going beyond father to beloved involve, in fact, quite different processes. While the woman has only to change the object of her affection, the man must change the gender of his. That a male is the object of Percy's desires is indicated not only in the Hermit scenes of *Islam* but in much of his life. If we compare the duration and intensity of Percy's bonds with men and with women, we may well agree with various scholars that the paramount figures of his emotional life are Hogg, Byron, Edward John Trelawny, and Edward Williams. Men are also the paramount objects when rage is the prevailing emotion. Inadequate fathers—Sir Timothy, Godwin, Wordsworth, Rousseau—obsess the poet-son to the end, to *The Triumph of Life*. Either way, rage or affection, the lesson is the same. Either solidarity with father is achieved, and woman is superfluous; or solidarity is denied, and the son's continued search for father keeps woman secondary.

Islam proves subversive in a different way if we view it in light of the Erotic desire for self-union which is a paramount theme of Percy Shelley and of *Frankenstein*. Is even a father-son bond possible? Male solidarity obviously constitutes a threatening alternative to self-union because the father becomes a rival who must be extirpated. But solidarity is even more threatening than that. It *fosters* death. Initially the son's escape from mother and body may be directed toward father and mind, but soon he recognizes that father is not only *as* mortal as mother and thus as incapable of assuring the son's immortality, father is *more* mortal. Uniting with him involves death as a precondition rather than simply as a consequence. Equality means mortality, since the son can ascend to the father's place upon the wheel of time only if he acknowledges the elder's humanity and thus accepts the inevitability of his own descent to death. Father is the ultimate threat to self-union because he provides a model so attractive that the son may accept mortality to achieve it.

There is something else about father, however, something promising for Eros. Father *in death* seems to offer an escape from mortality that mother, dead or alive, can not. So important is this aspect of father-son relations that it informs the major literary productions of both Mary and Percy Shelley.

II. Subversion and the Oedipus

I want to begin my discussion of Victor and his father Alphonse in what may seem an unlikely place—the Arab Maid of Shelley's *Alastor*. Mary in the opening frame of *Frankenstein* establishes her position on father-son conflicts by having Margaret Saville agree with Mr. Walton about the foolhardiness of Robert's seaborne quests. Since no one in the central frame of *Frankenstein* can succeed Margaret as arbiter, Mary proceeds more indirectly. In *Alastor*, the Arab Maid does what Mary considers natural and what she herself did for Percy—steals away from the father and tends upon the beloved. Woman's reward in *Alastor* is abandonment. "Self-centered seclusion" makes the male too obsessed with his "antitype" to bond with his complement. *Frankenstein* recapitulates the Arab Maid scenario, twice. "The Arabian," Safie, leaves her father and travels to Felix's home. Her reward is felicity. Elizabeth travels from her father to Frankenstein's home. Her reward is murder. The contrast between Felix's and Victor's treatments of woman signals that something is seriously wrong with Victor's relationship with father.

Felix, despite many hardships, feels no apparent antagonism toward a father excellent like the best old men in Mary's and Percy's art. Like the blind seer in Percy's "The Coliseum," M. De Lacey responds positively to the wanderer who comes seeking knowledge and love; like the Hermits in *Islam* and *Valperga*, he is served devotedly by an excellent daughter. With this ideal father, Felix achieves the solidarity which allows him, like Neville, to go on to complementary union with the beloved. Why can't Victor do the same with Alphonse and Elizabeth?

Critics in recent years have found oedipal tensions in the Victor-Alphonse relationship. They note that the son is hurt by his father's belittling Agrippa; that Victor consequently fears to share with Alphonse his new readings in alchemy and his later experiments in monster-making; that Victor feels exiled from the family when he is sent to Ingolstadt; that he associates Alphonse with the monster after Henry's murder; that he feels bound to his parents "by a silken cord" and includes "seemed" in his description of their love for him. These and other pieces of evidence fit so readily into psychoanalytic patterns that we can forget we are dealing with a character, not a patient. Especially since the text is a *narrator's* account, we must ascertain the *author's* intent. "When I would account to myself for the birth of that passion . . . I find . . ." Victor is accounting to himself. What "I find" is self-justification. Events which some psychoanalytic readers have taken as factual evidence may be convenient pretexts, as Kaplan and Kloss demonstrate with Victor's initial horror at the creature.

Why should Frankenstein react in this astounding way? . . . because the creature is ugly in appearance! At least this is the only explanation Frankenstein gives us.

But what an achievement is here. Ugly or not, it moves, breathes, lives! . . . With the description he gives, he might just as easily, and more realistically, have marvelled that the resemblance to a man was so close.

If we are to understand him, and the novel as well, we must presume that this terror, having its origin in other causes, is transferred to a convenient pretext.

Convenient pretexts are Victor's stock-in-trade. Particularly in passages defining the reasons for his behavior, Frankenstein's reactions often seem inordinate, the effects disproportionate to the causes. As we seek underlying motives, we must look carefully at Victor's placement of the blame upon Alphonse, and also at Levine's less extreme judgment that "fathers and sons are almost equally responsible and ir-responsible." We must, in other words, remain alive to distinctions between narrator and author, between Victor's assertion and our experience of it.

Take, for example, Alphonse's remark about Agrippa:

> My father looked carelessly at the title-page of my book, and said, "Ah! Cornelius Agrippa! My dear Victor, do not waste your time upon this; it is sad trash."
>
> If, instead of this remark, my father had taken the pains to explain to me, that the principles of Agrippa had been entirely exploded, and that a modern system of science had been introduced . . . , I should certainly have thrown Agrippa aside.

Victor is correct: Alphonse should explain, not simply dismiss. But just an unquestionably, the *magnitude* of Alphonse's failure is relevant too. Is our experience really that "a rationalist, like Godwin, the elder Frankenstein rather cruelly chastens his son's youthful imagination" [Knoepflmacher]? Alphonse's " 'my dear' " is neither rationalistic nor cruel, as Godwin's chastenings of Mary show. She could easily have made Alphonse's dismissal of Agrippa seem cruel enough to warrant Victor's reaction. Instead what we experience is a minor mistake. What parent has not missed by at least this much the proper tone in a random moment? (And random the moment is: on vacation, on a rainy day indoors, with a child who has never before envinced an interest in science.)

That Victor is finding convenient pretexts is signaled in his admission that "if, instead of this remark, my father had taken the pains to explain . . . I . . . should probably have applied myself to the more rational theory of chemistry which has resulted from modern discoveries. It is even possible, that the train of my ideas would never have received the fatal impulse that led to my ruin." Is it really? "Probably" and "possible" foster suspicions which are confirmed when Alphonse *does* explain about modern science.

> The catastrophe of this tree [hit by lightning] excited my extreme astonishment; and I eagerly inquired of my father the nature and origin of thunder and lightning. He replied, "Electricity"; describing at the same time the various effects of that power. He constructed a small electrical machine, and exhibited a few experiments; he made also a kite, with a wire and string, which drew down that fluid from the clouds.
>
> This last stroke completed the overthrow of Cornelius Agrippa.

Is our experience of this passage actually that the "1818 version of the novel is even harsher on the old man" than the substantially revised 1831 text, or that "Alphonse is also blamed for leading his son to science when he conducts a Franklin-like experiment" [Knoepflmacher]? Alphonse can't win for trying. Here he does all that Victor faulted him for omitting before: he is patient; he explains; he even demonstrates. How does Mary treat him harshly here? Or rather, what does it mean that "the 1818 version of the novel" treats him harshly? Is the treatment attributable to the author or to the narrator? That *Victor* is trying to implicate Alphonse in his youthful swerve toward destructive studies is clear. But we must distinguish between Victor's attempt and Mary's, between Victor's attempt and our response.

After the Franklin-like experiment, Victor "by some fatality . . . did not feel inclined to commence the study of any modern system." In its vagueness, "some fatality" carries on from "probably" and "possible," but it goes beyond these words as the clearest signal yet that the prime force operating upon Victor is not Alphonse. The 1818 edition introduces at this point a lecture course which "some accident" prevents Victor from attending "until the course was nearly finished. The lecture . . . was entirely incomprehensible to me." Accidents are convenient pretexts for Victor so often that we are not inclined to see external forces operating strongly here, and this interpretation is confirmed by Mary's revision in the 1831 edition of *Frankenstein*. The lecture course is deleted, Alphonse is replaced as Victor's electricity mentor by "a man of great research,"—and still the boy does not go on to study modern science.

> By some fatality the overthrow of these men [Agrippa, Albertus Magnus, Paracelsus] disinclined me to pursue my accustomed [scientific] studies. It seemed to me as if nothing would or could ever be known. All that had so long engaged my attention suddenly grew despicable. By one of those caprices of the mind . . . In this mood of mind I betook myself to the mathematics . . .
>
> Thus strangely are our souls constructed . . . Destiny was too potent, and her immutable laws had decreed my utter and terrible destruction.

By repeating the word "fatality," which begs the question that it seems to answer, Mary directs us away from Alphonse and toward Victor. "It seemed to me" . . . "suddenly" . . . "caprices of the mind"

. . . "mood of mind " . . . "strangely" . . . "Destiny" . . . "Laws had decreed." Victor does not understand what is happening inside him and does not want to. Mary, I believe, tries to avoid in 1831 exactly what Dussinger faults her for—"indecisiveness" about Alphonse's role in 1818. Having initially established that Victor's "family was not scientifical," Mary needed the boy familiarized with modern science and she chose Alphonse as the handiest teacher—forgetting that he was not scientifical. Later, in the Thomas copy, she caught her mistake and reminded herself in the margin "you said your family was not scientific." In 1831 she corrects the mistake by keeping Alphonse consistently nonscientifical and inventing, clumsily, the man of great research who teaches Victor what she wants him to know. Mary never, I feel, intended a rivalry between Alphonse and Victor as scientists, never intended the father to have any large role in the son's disastrous move toward monster-making. Father and son do not seem almost equally responsible and irresponsible. Instead the son absolves himself of irresponsibility by making the father responsible.

To appreciate Victor's motivation here, we must, I feel, heed a distinction present in Freud and important in recent psychoanalytic work—a distinction between the Oedipus as a fantasy projected by the son upon the innocent father and the Oedipus as a son's correct perception about the father. Psychoanalytic critics have tended to assume that the latter is the case in *Frankenstein*, whereas I incline to the former. Victor blames Alphonse for sending him to Ingolstadt, for example.

> When I had attained the age of seventeen, my parents resolved that I should become a student at the university of Ingolstadt. I had hitherto attended the schools of Geneva; but my father thought it necessary, for the completion of my education, that I should be made acquainted with other customs than those of my native country. My departure was therefore fixed at an early date.

"I" *attain* seventeen, but the family does the rest. "My parents resolved" . . . "my father thought" . . . "my departure was therefore fixed." The son is already feeling himself driven from home and mother by his rival the father (and may also be feeling, as the plural "parents" indicates, that mother is siding with father) when suddenly Caroline Frankenstein dies. What ensues is analyzed well by Dussinger. Victor first blames his mothers's death on his father's banishing of him; then Alphonse's continued insistence upon Victor's departure makes the son see things the opposite way—that the father blames *him* for Caroline's death and is punishing him with banishment. "The narrator, it would be possible to say, wants to lessen his guilt involved in his secret rebellion against the enervating domestic order by attributing the decision to leave to his father." Victor's word "early" supports Dussinger by indicating not only that the date is soon, but that the son feels it is too soon, feels he is being forced to leave early. This is not how we take it, however. That sons become "acquainted with other customs than those of . . . [their] native country" is a traditional goal of fathers. Particularly in Mary's fiction, sons repeatedly practice the wisdom preached in *Lodore:* " 'At seventeen years many their fortunes seek.' " At "seventeen" Lodore goes off to Oxford; Lionel, admonished by Adrian in *The Last Man* to "begin life . . . you are seventeen," sets off for "the necessary apprenticeship" in a foreign land. And barely a month before her seventeen birthday, Mary Godwin elopes with Percy Shelley.

The contrast between Victor's reluctance and the eagerness of Castruccio, whose "fervent desire" as "he entered his seventeenth year" was "to quit what he thought a lifeless solitude," shows how closely Victor resembles Percy Shelley [*Valperga*]. Percy, who at various times suspected Sir Timothy of seeking to exile him to a madhouse and the Peninsular Wars, sees the inevitable need to go away to school as a father-generated plan of banishment. *He* responds by setting a washroom fire which could have consumed his home.

The parallels with Percy's life and the analogues in Mary's fiction confirm our sense that Alphonse is not malevolent, especially since he sympathetically postpones Victor's departure after Caroline's death. Victor downplays the sympathy by mitigating Alphonse's agency. "I obtained from my father a respite of some weeks." The emphasis is upon "I." That what I do is to "obtain," and "a respite" stresses the son's subservience and his struggle to wrest a concession from father. The truly domineering father in *Frankenstein* is M. Clerval, who for a long time forbids Henry to attend Ingolstadt. Why would Mary portray Henry's father this way except to highlight Victor's father? Instead of the psychological pattern which Frankenstein implies—that Alphonse's traditional goal and sympathetic postponement of it screen his "real," oedipal design—we experience the well-intentioned plan of a father properly ambitious for his gifted son.

Where does Victor get an "oedipal" sense of father-son relations nearly a century before Freud? The obvious answer—that sons have ever felt abused by fathers—is bolstered by a more historiographic source. Gothic fiction, as Judith Wilt argues, makes paternal abuse a major theme. "The son must die so that the old man may live." This paradigm, which recurs from *The Castle of Otranto* through *Dracula*, is prominent in Godwin's *Caleb Williams* and *St. Leon*. In *Frankenstein*, however, the son's oppression by the father informs not the plot of the novel but the mind of the protagonist: Victor interprets life as though it were a Gothic novel. Mary Shelley dramatizes not the oedipal paranoia of the Gothic tradition but the dangers of such paranoia, the dangers of approaching complex realities with the self-justifying convenience of a paradigm. *Frankenstein* is, in this sense, anti-Gothic. It is orthodoxy's counterattack against the dark tradition which had exposed the self-deceived convenience of its own sentimental paradigms. In another sense, however, Mary's very skepticism about Gothic paranoia is very Gothic. Monk Lewis, Charles Maturin, James Hogg, Thomas Lovell Beddoes, as well as Brown, Edgar Allan Poe, Nathaniel Hawthorne, and Herman Melville all share her distrust of the son's self-justifying rage, even as they, like her, make oedipal emotions central to their art. Mary Shelley's critical examination of all paradigms, Gothic and sentimental, is what drives her and her readers beyond Victor's self-justifying explanations to the darker teleology of him and Percy.

III. The Negative Oedipus

What is the nature of the antagonism toward Alphonse which Victor expresses in oedipal terms? Psychoanalytic critics have rightly seen Victor's philanthropic rationale for monster-making as a convenient pretext. The claim that he is creating life in order to save mankind from death screens Frankenstein's deeper desire to resuscitate his dead mother. Readers can, however, recognize this second level and still sense another, even deeper motive. Victor's devotion to woman is not all it might be. He kills woman. As a wish fulfillment, Victor's famous nightmare is manifestly *not* oedipal because the nightmare kiss functions not to awaken the mother from death, as in "Sleeping Beauty," but to reduce Elizabeth to Caroline's moribund state. Victor is then free to move beyond woman to father. In Freudian terms, Victor's feelings are not oedipal (kill the father to possess the mother) but negative oedipal (kill the mother to possess the father).

Why father? The answer, as we have seen, cannot lie in any illusion of paternal immortality. In fact one reason why Percy rages against old men is that he too is aging, and prematurely. When he says "I have lived to be older than my father," he is reflecting not only upon his superior wisdom but upon his graying hair and wasted body. Confronted with the danger of becoming *like* his father, Percy determines to *become* his father.

This determination is proclaimed, quite amazingly, on the title pages of his first two books of verse. *Original Poetry* is authored by Victor (Percy) and Cazire (Elizabeth Shelley); *Posthumous Fragments of Margaret Nicholson* is "edited" by John Fitzvictor. Victor and Fitzvictor. What Shelley desired ultimately is not what *Islam* idealized, not that place upon the wheel of time which allows to both son and father the dignity of all roles from birth to death. Victor and Fitzvictor, father and son: Shelley desires to become his own father because as Victor-Fitzvictor he can sire himself.

How this promises immortality is dramatized in *Prometheus Unbound*. Demogorgon is eternal. Like Percy, he is older than his father, but unlike Percy, he is not threatened by age. This son who kills the father lives forever. Demogorgon who descends as Killer-Son with Jupiter in act 2 emerges by himself as Eternity in act 4. He is no longer "son" because he no longer has a father. Even as fantasy, however, Demogorgon seems unsatisfying: since Shelley is not eternal, how can he take Demogorgon for his model? The answer to this question lies in Percy's understanding of myth. Demogorgon's association with Eternity comes not from Thomas Love Peacock or John Milton but from Boccaccio. In *The Genealogy of the Pagan Gods*, Demogorgon is the principle of force who cohabits with the Witch of Eternity. Shelley takes this union of male and female and combines the two principles into one character. Demogorgon ingests the female principle of eternity. If Shelley can do likewise, if he can contain both masculine and feminine as self and antitype, he can become self-sufficient.

Like the snake swallowing its tail, the male can provide both the phallus and its receptacle. Siring oneself assures immortality by closing the generative cycle and thus precluding death. Victor-Fitzvictor. For this most perversely solipsistic version of his antitype idea, Percy finds sanctioning precedents in both Romantic satanism and orthodox Christianity. One of the things which attracts the Romantics to Milton's Satan is his daring claim to self-generation. This parodies the Christian notion that "the Father pours himself out into the son; the son, knowing himself separate, makes the astonishing choice to curve that stream of being back toward the progenitor" [Wilt]. Victor's discovery of the secret of life abolishes Alphonse by supplanting the very biological process which made the father a father. Rather than curve the stream of being back to Alphonse, Frankenstein as the only begetter of a new system of begetting curves it into himself.

Although Frankenstein's desire to become Fitz-victor is achieved partially by giving birth to himself as monster, he remains a son so long as he, like Demogorgon, has a father. Alphonse must die. Mary's *Frankenstein* and Percy's life and art thus feature early in the nineteenth century a motif recurrent in Western culture and particularly central to literature and biography for the next hundred and fifty years—sons desiring to extirpate fathers and to sire themselves. Both the desire and its consequences are summed up in Freud's essay on Dostoyevski: "You wanted to kill your father in order to be your father yourself. Now you *are* your father, but a dead father." Recent critics have found this motif in novelists as diverse as Melville ("behind these [Pierre's] strategems lies the desire to be one's own father") and Joyce ("Stephen is the son-type in the process of fathering himself"). In Dickens, Thackeray, and Faulkner, this process is made still more intricate by the son's attempt to recreate himself through language. Pip, "the metaphorical writer-as-son . . . attempts to give birth to himself in writing, to beget or engender himself without the help of fathers"; Esmond, "the fatherless son[,] is allowed, in a sense, to be father himself through the first-person narrative"; and Quentin can become in effect the sire of Jason Sr. if he can articulate the Compson history and thus "seize his father's authority by gaining temporal priority." Mary Shelley agrees emphatically with all these writers about "the lunacy of attempting . . . to engender the self," but the most relevant context for her masterpiece remains Percy Shelley. He provides Mary with an immediate example of that "poetic will," that reaction against father and that concern with self-generation which characterize the next two hundred years and which have been called by Harold Bloom "an argument against time, revengefully seeking no substitute 'It is' for 'it was.' Yet this argument always splits in two, because the poetic will needs to make another outrageous substitution, of 'I am' for 'It is.' Both parts of the argument are quests for priority."

In the analysis which follows I will often discuss Victor in terms of works written by Percy *after* 1818. Two considerations warrant this. As Percy's "handwriting was very early formed and never altered," so the artistic products of that hand show remarkable consistency [Thomas Medwin, *The Life of Percy Bysshe Shelly*]. The dismissal of the living Godwin as dead in the 1820 "Letter to Maria Gisborne" repeats the 1815 dismissal of Wordsworth which I will discuss soon. More important, the psychological moves I will define in *Prometheus Unbound* and *The Cenci*—the dual need to assassinate and to deny responsibility for the act—repeat at the highest levels of art what Percy had been doing at least since he introduced plagiarism into *Original Poetry* and then blamed Elizabeth Shelley for it. Victor in 1818 can anticipate Percy's moves in 1819 because Mary has learned through grim experience her husband's instinctual responses. In the intricate literary interaction between *Frankenstein* and *Prometheus Unbound* and *The Cenci*, it is as though Percy learns from Mary what he had taught her. Or rather, he reaffirms in 1819 what she had urged him in 1818 to repudiate.

Fundamental to the Greek myth of Prometheus is father-killing. Jupiter destroyed his sire, Saturn, and was in turn threatened by his own offspring. Attractive as this situation is to the Erotic Percy, it does not lead to the absolute annihilation he requires. "The *Prometheus Unbound* of Aeschylus supposed the reconciliation of Jupiter with his victim . . . I was averse from a catastrophe so feeble as that of reconciling the Champion with the Oppressor of mankind." Reconciliation was the theme of *Islam* and *Prince Athanase*, but father, like almost everything else with Percy, evokes contradictory responses. While *Islam* revealed the ideal acceptance of paternal manhood which Agape encourages, other poems express the Erotic son's attack upon the manhood of sires who have failed to measure up. Percy finds it difficult to discover limitations in an authority figure and still acknowledge that man's masculinity. Wordsworth is a "moral eunuch" in *Peter Bell the Third*, "an unsexual man" (ll. 314, 551). Percy cannot face directly the sexuality of that ultimate elder, Sir Timothy, so he strikes back by claiming superior maturity. " 'I have lived to be older than my father, I am ninety years of age' "; " 'The life of a man of talent who should die in his *thirtieth year*, is, with regard to his own feelings, longer than that of a miserable priest-ridden slave' " [Medwin]. Although Percy credits himself here with that experiential wisdom which Laon and Prince Athanase acceded to, his life cannot achieve what *Islam* and *Prince Athanase* enacted—the friendship between younger and older male which assures their equality and manhood.

Unable to be reconciled to Wordsworth or Godwin or Sir Timothy,

Percy Shelley never resolves his obsession with fathers. Instead he extirpates them.

> Deserting these [truth and liberty], thou leavest me to grieve,
> Thus having been, that thou shouldst cease to be.
> ("To Wordsworth," ll. 13–14)

Needless to say, Wordsworth is very much alive in 1815. But not to Percy. Unlike *Islam* where the limitations of the elder male could be acknowledged and accepted, "To Wordsworth" tolerates no deviation from the ideal. Once Wordsworth acts as he should not, he ceases to be. The same happens to Godwin. With a switch of verb tense and a switch to neuter gender, Percy can switch off a man whose life has failed to measure up:

> [In London] . . . You [the Gisbornes] will see
> That which was Godwin . . .
>
> .   .   .   .
>
> You will see Coleridge—he who sits obscure.
> ("Letter to Maria Gisborne," ll. 196–97, 202)

And Sir Timothy? Again Percy finds its hardest to deal with his real father, but again he manages to make his point. The need to defeat rather than to bond with father shapes both of Percy's greatest long works.

As *Islam* idealized the reconciliation advocated by Agape, *Prometheus Unbound* effects the extermination required by Eros. Percy transforms father from loving Hermit to Jupiter, the quintessential evil. The son's response to him is not the guilt-producing one of a patricide but the noble one of an assassin. What might seem self-indulgent becomes obligatory: the world must be redeemed from Evil.

This change cannot preclude guilt entirely, so Percy further justifies assassination by aligning himself with two of the canonical traditions of his time. As Romantic, he models his rejection of reconciliation upon the heroic defiance of Satan in *Paradise Lost*. Satan is, however, hardly a model to all readers (or to Percy as erstwhile Christian), so the poet acknowledges the "ambition, envy, revenge" of Milton's character and makes Jesus Christ another of his own party. "Christ the benevolent champion, falsely identified with the Son of God, must destroy the notion of the Father in the mind of Man in order to vindicate his own humanity and goodness" [William H. Marshall, "The Father-Child Symbolism in *Prometheus Unbound*," *Modern Language Quarterly* 22

(March 1961)]. Since guilt still remains a possibility so long as killing remains the theme, Percy makes the ultimate gesture and declares Prometheus perfect—"the type of the highest perfection of moral and intellectual nature, impelled by the purest and the truest motives to the best and noblest ends."

An apparently insuperable dilemma now confronts Percy: either someone perfect cannot kill, or a killer cannot be perfect. The way out of this dilemma is explained by Mary herself. "According to the mythological story . . . the offspring of Thetis . . . was destined to be greater than his father. . . . Shelley adapted the catastrophe of this story to his peculiar views. The son greater than his father . . . was to dethrone Evil." In Percy's "peculiar" view, the "son" is *two* men who reflect his contradictory responses to father. Prometheus is Percy the son who, though oppressed by fathers, remains as perfect in love as they are sunk in evil. Then, since the "son" in the Greek myth is not Prometheus, the actual offspring of Thetis can express homicidal rage. Demogorgon does what Percy-Prometheus cannot and what Percy-Assassin must. Demogorgon does the dirty work and keeps Prometheus's hands clean.

Deflection of guilt occurs in a different way in *The Cenci*. Father is again made so monstrously evil that no substantial sympathy can devolve to him, and the agent of assassination is again removed sufficiently from Percy (Beatrice is female and modeled from life) to prevent his direct implication. To make all the more certain that guilt cannot surface, Percy resorts to another characteristic expedient—indignation. He criticizes the woman who does his bidding, as he blamed his sister Elizabeth for his plagiarism in *Original Poetry*.

> Undoubtedly, no person can be truly dishonoured by the act of another; and the fit return to make to the most enormous injuries is kindness and forbearance, and a resolution to convert the injurer from his dark passions by peace and love. Revenge, retaliation, atonement, are pernicious mistakes. If Beatrice had thought in this manner she would have been wiser and better.

My point is not to contest the moral stance taken in the *Cenci* preface ("turn the other cheek" is impeccably Christian), or to belabor the fact that Percy did not always turn the cheek when his was the one struck (as in the Rhine boat incident of 1814, the Rome Post Office fight of 1819, and the Pisa fracas of 1822). My point is the priggish inflexibility of the preface's attitude toward Beatrice. A man who assures a woman that rape does not really touch her essence and that she must submit to whatever degradations lie ahead—this man should employ warier rhetoric. The lack of syntactic complication in "if Beatrice had thought in this [my] manner, she would have been wiser and better" contrasts with the manifold complications of Beatrice's actual situation. She cannot escape the house; no one would shelter her anyway; and her father will unquestionably carry out his threat to rape her again and again. Percy's sentence, however, is not badly written. Its syntactic stiffness and righteous tone are the inevitable consequences of its therapeutic—as opposed to its rhetorical—purpose. Its function is not only, or at least not primarily, to persuade us that Beatrice acted wrongly, but also to convince Percy that he feels properly. Percy guiltily uses the preface to insist upon the proper attitude toward patricide, after his unconscious has already used the play to satisfy homicidal desires. Readers of the play empathize consistently with Beatrice because the Erotic Percy enjoys her patricide. She is, after all, destroying Sir Timothy, and Godwin, and Wordsworth, and . . .

That Alphonse evokes comparable conflicts in Victor is revealed in the conflict between Victor's surrogate, the monster, and Alphonse's youngest son, William.

> "Hideous monster! Let me [William] go; My papa is a Syndic—he is M. Frankenstein . . ."
> "Frankenstein! You belong then to my enemy . . . you shall be my first victim."

William is doomed only when he is identified as a son; murder was not inevitable or apparently even intended before that. Victor's first strike at Alphonse is thus through his beloved son. (This son in turn warrants punishment as a sibling rival for the father's affection, and for the mother's love too, since William is in possession of Caroline's portrait. Emblematic of Victor's sense of domestic exclusion is the fact that when word of William's death calls him back to Geneva, "the gates of the town were already shut." The traditional association of "little brother" and penis emphasizes the castrating intent of striking at the father through his offspring. As an indirect move, it saves Victor from having to lay a guilt-fostering hand upon the father. Since the act *is* indirect, however, since little William is only a stand-in for Alphonse, a second attack must be launched against the now vulnerable sire. Frankenstein must assassinate Alphonse to become a true victor.

The guilt and awe generated by patricide continue to require that the son proceed indirectly, so Victor resorts to both of the tactics practiced by Shelley in his long poems. As Shelley displaced his dark deeds upon another (Demogorgon, Beatrice Cenci, and Elizabeth Shelley), Victor has created the monster to enact his murderous will against his family. His hands remain legally as clean as Prometheus's. In fact the monster does not even dirty *his* hands with Alphonse's blood. The creature could have swum across the lake and throttled the unsuspecting sire before Victor reached Geneva to warn him, but this would have brought patricide too close to home. The most fiendish thing about the sequence of events generated by Frankenstein's Erotic unconscious is that it results—in effect—in Alphonse's suicide. By succumbing to grief, the old man dies of natural causes, and lets Victor off Shelley-free. The son does remain conscience-ridden, however. "An apoplectic fit was brought on." *By whom*, the sentence cannot admit. The question of responsibility, of agency, need not even have come up, had not guilt at killing by indirection prompted the self-indicting Victor to forego the active construction ("he died of an apoplectic fit") which would have acquitted him entirely.

To emphasize his innocence, Victor further deflects guilt through indignation. Like Percy in the *Cenci* preface, he vilifies his surrogate. In fact-to-face encounters, he accuses the monster of having " 'diabolically murdered' " innocent " 'victims' "; and in a retrospective move like that of Percy's preface, he concludes that the creature "shewed unparalleled malignity and selfishness." Since this is society's reaction (everyone abhors the monster), and since this would surely be Alphonse's reaction (you have slaughtered my children), Victor's indignation testifies to his orthodoxy as Percy's indignation did in the *Cenci* preface.

Even if Victor's need for clean hands precludes the monster's throttling Alphonse, grief over little William and Justine (and Caroline) could have caused Alphonse to die conventionally from sorrow *before* Elizabeth's murder. The unconvincing thing about fictional deaths-from-sorrow is precisely that they can occur whenever the novelist requires. Why does Mary Shelley require so many corpses, and why is Alphonse's death the last?

William   Justine   Henry   Elizabeth   Alphonse

The deaths proceed in terms of increasingly important relationships for Victor: a tie with a child, then with a peer, then with the closest male peer, then with the still closer female peer, and finally the ultimate bond with father. With each increase of intimacy, there is a greater threat to the self-union which promises immortality. And, as we have seen, father is the supreme threat because solidarity with him is an alternate ideal. " 'Whose death,' cried I, 'is to finish the tragedy? Ah! my father, do not remain in this wretched country.' " Victor's covert message—" 'to finish . . . my father' "—solves the problem it poses: " 'the tragedy . . . my father.' " Victor at some deep level knows the teleology that he will not acknowledge. Mary stresses Alphonse's climactic placement in the family fatalities by having Victor say in 1831 "I turned to contemplate the deep and voiceless grief of my Elizabeth. This also was my doing! And my father's woe." Victor knows. After Elizabeth's "voiceless" death by strangulation comes the father's death from "woe."

But there is more. As the last fatality, Alphonse fits not only in a scale of increasing intimacy but also into a reversal of alphabetical order.

W–J–H–E–A

Whether Mary consciously intended to reverse alphabetization—and for an author attentive to names to do it accidentally seems unlikely to me—the fact of the reversal reflects her reaction to self-union. The reversal establishes that Victor's motion to father is regressive. "Regressive" can mean two things. Insofar as Victor-Percy is capable of the intimacy and solidarity of Agape, regressive has the positive associations of the term in Freud's clinical papers (particularly "Remembering, Repeating, and Working-Through") and in more recent discussions of transference (particularly by Jacques Lacan and Heinz Kohut). The analysand cannot simply be *told* what is the matter; s/he must work back to the original trauma and either reexperience it or experience a comparable moment through the transference. If this were what Victor was attempting, if he were returning to his childhood relationship with Alphonse in order to understand and relive it, then "regression" would mean that the son was making the peace with the parent which is essential if psychological and social maturity is to match biological development. Particularly if we see the father in light of *Totem and Taboo* and the work of Lacan, Phallus as Law is what the son should be oriented to. Victor's pursuit of the monster could then signal a therapeutically male orientation. But since Victor pursues the monster with unnatural attraction and homicidal rage, and since his own father is ultimately absent because Victor has killed him, "regressive" has the negative connotations of ordinary parlance.

W–J–H–E–A. After "A" there is nothing else. It is the beginning as end, Alpha as Omega of I AM. Suppose Mary had named Victor's father Bartholomew or Benedict or Bardolph. Suppose, in other words, that after Mother—Caroline—and Father—Bardolph—there remained *A*. Son would have some role beyond, before family. But Father is the end of the line. Beyond Mother there is Alphonse, but beyond Alphonse—Alpha—there is only silence. In his desire to become Victor-Fitzvictor, in his determination to predate his predecessor and sire himself, Frankenstein has regressed from society to preexistence, to the letterless wordless tundra of the phallic Pole's self-centered seclusion.

Bearing Demons: Frankenstein's Circumvention of the Maternal

Margaret Homans

Married to one Romantic poet and living near another, Mary Shelley at the time she was writing *Frankenstein* experienced with great intensity the self-contradictory demand that daughters embody both the mother whose death makes language possible by making it necessary and the figurative substitutes for that mother who constitute the prototype of the signifying chain. At the same time, as a mother herself, she experienced with far greater intensity than did any of the authors considered so far a proto-Victorian ideology of motherhood, as Mary Poovey has shown. This experience leads Shelley both to figure her writing as mothering and to bear or transmit the words of her husband. Thus Shelley not only practices the daughter's obligatory and voluntary identification with the literal, as do Dorothy Wordsworth and Charlotte and Emily Brontë, but she also shares with George Eliot and Elizabeth Gaskell (and again with Charlotte Brontë) their concern with writing as literalization, as a form of mothering. It is to Shelley's handling of these contradictory demands, and to her criticism of their effect on women's writing, that my reading of *Frankenstein* will turn.

Frankenstein portrays the situation of women obliged to play the role of the literal in a culture that devalues it. In this sense, the novel is simultaneously about the death and obviation of the mother and about the son's quest for a substitute object of desire. The novel criticizes the

From *Bearing the Word: Language and Female Experience in Nineteenth-Century Women's Writing.* © 1986 by the University of Chicago. University of Chicago Press, 1986.

self-contradictory male requirement that that substitute at once embody and not embody (because all embodiment is a reminder of the mother's powerful and forbidden body) the object of desire. The horror of the demon that Frankenstein creates is that it is the literalization of its creator's desire for an object, a desire that never really seeks its own fulfillment.

Many readers of *Frankenstein* have noted both that the demon's creation amounts to an elaborate circumvention of normal heterosexual procreation—Frankenstein does by himself with great difficulty what a heterosexual couple can do quite easily—and that each actual mother dies very rapidly upon being introduced as a character in the novel. Frankenstein's own history is full of the deaths of mothers. His mother was discovered, as a poverty-stricken orphan, by Frankenstein's father. Frankenstein's adoptive sister and later fiancée, Elizabeth, was likewise discovered as an orphan, in poverty, by Frankenstein's parents. Elizabeth catches scarlet fever, and her adoptive mother, nursing her, catches it herself and dies of it. On her deathbed, the mother hopes for the marriage of Elizabeth and Frankenstein and tells Elizabeth, "You must supply my place to my younger children" (chap. 3). Like Shelley herself, Elizabeth is the death of her mother and becomes a substitute for her. Justine, a young girl taken in by the Frankenstein family as a beloved servant, is said to cause the death of her mother; and Justine herself, acting as foster mother to Frankenstein's little brother, William, is executed for his murder. There are many mothers in the Frankenstein circle, and all die notable deaths.

The significance of the apparently necessary destruction of the mother first emerges in Frankenstein's account of his preparations for creating the demon, and it is confirmed soon after the demon comes to life. Of his early passion for science, Frankenstein says, "I was . . . deeply smitten with the thirst for knowledge" (chap. 2). Shelley confirms the oedipal suggestion here when she writes that it is despite his father's prohibition that the young boy devours the archaic books on natural philosophy that first raise his ambitions to dicover the secret of life. His mother dies just as Frankenstein is preparing to go to the University of Ingolstadt, and if his postponed trip there is thus motivated by her death, what he finds at the university becomes a substitute for her: modern scientists, he is told, "penetrate into the recesses of nature and show how she works in her hiding-places" (chap. 3). Frankenstein's double, Walton, the polar explorer who rescues him and records his story, likewise searches for what sound like sexual secrets, also in violation of a paternal prohibition. Seeking to "satiate [his] ardent curiosity," Walton hopes to find the "wondrous power which attracts the needle" (letter 1). Frankenstein, having become "capable of bestowing animation upon lifeless matter," feels that to arrive "at once at the summit of my desires was the most gratifying consummation of my toils." And his work to create the demon adds to this sense of an oedipal violation of Mother Nature: dabbling "among the unhallowed damps of the grave," he "disturbed, with profane fingers, the tremendous secrets of the human frame" (chap. 4). This violation is necrophiliac. The mother he rapes is dead; his researches into her secrets, to usurp her powers, require that she be dead.

Frankenstein describes his violation of nature in other ways that recall what William Wordsworth's poetry reveals when read in conjunction with Dorothy Wordsworth's journals. Of the period during which he is working on the demon, Frankenstein writes,

> The summer months passed while I was thus engaged, heart and soul, in one pursuit. It was a most beautiful season; never did the fields bestow a more plentiful harvest or the vines yield a more luxuriant vintage, but my eyes were insensible to the charms of nature. . . . Winter, spring, and summer passed away during my labours; but I did not watch the blossom or the expanding leaves—sights which before always yielded me supreme delight—so deeply was I engrossed in my occupation.
>
> (chap. 4)

Ignoring the bounteous offering nature makes of itself and substituting for it his own construction of life, what we, following Thomas Wieskel, might call his own reading of nature, Frankenstein here resembles William Wordsworth, reluctantly and ambivalently allowing himself to read nature, to impose on nature apocalyptic patterns of meaning that destroy it. Dorothy Wordsworth herself makes an appearance in the text of Frankenstein, if indirectly, and her presence encodes a shared women's critique of the Romantic reading of nature. Much later in the novel, Frankenstein compares his friend Clerval to the former self William Wordsworth depicts in "Tintern Abbey," a self that he has outgrown but that his sister remains. Shelley quotes (with one major alteration) the lines beginning, "The sounding cataract / Haunted him like a passion" and ending with the assertion that the colors and forms of natural objects (rock, mountain, etc.) were

> a feeling, and a love,
> That had no need of a remoter charm,
> By thought supplied, or any interest
> Unborrow'd from the eye.

If Clerval is like Dorothy, then Frankenstein is like William, regrettably destroying nature by imposing his reading on it.

When, assembled from the corpse of nature, the demon has been brought to life and Frankenstein has recognized—oddly only now that it is alive—how hideous it is, Frankenstein falls into an exhausted sleep and dreams the following dream:

> I thought I saw Elizabeth, in the bloom of health, walking in the streets of Ingolstadt. Delighted and surprised, I embraced her, but as I imprinted the first kiss on her lips, they became livid with the hue of death; her features appeared to change, and I thought that I held the corpse of my dead mother in my arms; a shroud enveloped her form, and I saw the grave-worms crawling in the folds of the flannel. I started from my sleep with horror.
>
> (chap. 5)

He wakes to see the demon looking at him, hideous, but clearly loving. The dream suggests that to bring the demon to life is equivalent to killing Elizabeth, and that Elizabeth dead is equivalent to his mother dead. Elizabeth may have been the death of the mother, but now that she has replaced her, she too is vulnerable to whatever destroys mothers. And, indeed, the dream is prophetic: the demon will much later kill Elizabeth, just as the demon's creation has required both the death of Frankenstein's own mother and the death and violation of Mother Nature. To bring a composite corpse to life is to circumvent the normal channels of procreation; the demon's "birth" violates the normal relations of family, especially the normal sexual relation of husband and wife. Victor has gone to great lengths to produce a child without Elizabeth's assistance, and in the dream's language, to circumvent her, to make her unnecessary, is to kill her, and to kill mothers altogether.

Frankenstein's creation, then, depends on and then perpetuates the death of the mother and of motherhood. The demon's final, and greatest, crime is in fact its murder of Elizabeth, which is, however, only the logical extension of its existence as the reification of Frankenstein's desire to escape the mother. The demon is, to borrow a phrase from Shelley's *Alastor*, "the spirit of" Frankenstein's "solitude." Its greatest complaint to Frankenstein is of its own solitude, its isolation from humanity, and it promises that if Frankenstein will make it a mate, "one as hideous as myself. . . . I shall become a thing of whose existence everyone will be ignorant" (chap. 17). That is, no longer solitary, the demon will virtually cease to exist, for its existence is synonymous with its solitude. But, on the grounds that "a race of devils would be propagated upon the earth," Frankenstein destroys the female demon he is in the process of creating, thus destroying yet another potential mother, and the demon promises, "I shall be with you on your wedding-night" (chap. 20). If the demon is the form taken by Frankenstein's flight from the mother, then it is impossible that the demon should itself find an embodied substitute for the mother, and it will prevent Frankenstein from finding one too.

The demon's promise to be present at the wedding night suggests that there is something monstrous about Frankenstein's sexuality. A solipsist's sexuality is monstrous because his desire is for his own envisionings rather than for somebody else, some other body. The demon appears where Frankenstein's wife should be, and its murder of her suggests not so much revenge as jealousy. The demon's murder of that last remaining potential mother makes explicit the sequel to the obviation of the mother, the male quest for substitutes for the mother, the quest that is never intended to be fulfilled. Elizabeth suggests in a letter to Frankenstein that his reluctance to marry may stem from his love for someone else, someone met, perhaps, in his travels or during his long stay in Ingolstadt. "Do you not love another?" she asks (chap. 22). This is in fact the case, for the demon, the creation of Frankenstein's imagination, resembles in many ways the Romantic object of desire, the beloved invented to replace, in a less threatening form, the powerful mother who must be killed. This imagined being would be an image of the self, because it is for the sake of the ego that the mother is rejected in the first place. Created right after the death of the mother to be, as Victor says, "a being like myself" (chap. 4), the demon may be Adam, created in God's image. Indeed, this is what the demon thinks when it tells Frankenstein, "I ought to be thy Adam, but I am rather the fallen angel" (chap. 10). But it is also possible, as Gilbert and Gubar suggest, that the demon is Eve, created from Adam's imagination.

When the demon takes shelter in the French cottager's shed, it looks, repeating Milton's Eve's first act upon coming to life, into the mirror of a "clear pool" and is terrified at its own reflection: "I started back" (chap. 12). Here is the relevant passage from Milton, from Eve's narration in book 4 of her memory of the first moments of her creation. Hearing the "murmuring sound / Of water issu'd from a Cave and spread / Into a liquid Plain," Eve looks

> into the clear
> Smooth Lake, that to me seem'd another Sky.
> As I bent down to look, just opposite,
> A Shape within the wat'ry gleam appear'd
> Bending to look on me, I started back,
> It started back, but pleas'd I soon return'd . . .
> (*Paradise Lost*, 4.453–63)

But the disembodied voice instructs her, "What there thou seest fair Creature is thyself" (468), and tells her to follow and learn to prefer him "whose image thou art" (471–72). Christine Froula argues that the fiction of Eve's creation by a paternal God out of the flesh of Adam values the maternal and appropriates it for the aggrandisement of masculine creativity ["When Eve Reads Milton: Undoing the Canonical Economy," in *Canons*, ed. Robert von Hallberg]. *Frankenstein* revises this paradigm for artistic creation: he does not so much appropriate the maternal as bypass it, to demonstrate the unnecessariness of natural motherhood and, indeed, of women. Froula points out that in this "scene of canonical instruction," Eve is required to turn away from herself to embrace her new identity, not as a self, but as the image of someone else. Created to the specifications of Adam's desire, we later learn—"Thy likeness, thy fit help, thy other self, / Thy wish, exactly to thy heart's desire" (8.450–51)—Eve is, like Frankenstein's demon, the product of imaginative desire. Milton appropriates the maternal by excluding any actual mother from the scene of creation. Eve is the form that Adam's desire takes once actual motherhood has been eliminated; and in much the same way, the demon is the form taken by Frankenstein's desire once his mother and Elizabeth as mother have been circumvented. These new creations in the image of the self are substitutes for the powerful creating mother and place creation under the control of the son.

That the demon is, like Eve, the creation of a son's imaginative desire is confirmed by another allusion both closer to Shelley and closer in the text to Elizabeth's question, "Do you not love another?" Mary Poovey has argued that the novel criticizes Romantic egotism, specifically, Percy Shelley's violation of the social conventions that bind humans together in families and societies. As the object of desire of an imaginative overreacher very like Percy Shelley himself, the demon substitutes for the fruitful interchange of family life the fruitlessness of self love, for what Frankenstein loves is an image of himself. The novel was written when Percy Shelley had completed, of all his major works besides *Queen Mab*, only *Alastor*, the archetypal poem of the doomed Romantic quest, and it is to this poem that Mary Shelley alludes. Just before Frankenstein receives Elizabeth's letter, just after being acquitted of the murder of his friend Clerval, Frankenstein tells us, "I saw around me nothing but a dense and frightful darkness, penetrated by no light but the glimmer of two eyes that glared upon me" (chap. 21). This is a direct allusion to a passage in *Alastor* in which the hero, who has quested in vain after an ideal female image of his own creation, sees

> two eyes,
> Two starry eyes, hung in the gloom of thought,
> And seemed with their serene and azure smiles
> To beckon him.
>
> (ll. 489–92)

In *Alastor*, these eyes belong to the phantom maiden, the "fleeting shade" whom the hero pursues to his death, a beloved who is constructed out of the poet's own visionary narcissism. The girl he dreams and pursues has a voice "like the voice of his own soul / Heard in the calm of thought" (ll. 153–54), and like him, she is "Herself a poet" (l. 161). In the novel, the starry eyes become glimmering, glaring eyes, alternately the eyes of the dead Clerval and the "watery, clouded eyes of the monster, as I first saw them in my chamber at Ingolstadt" (chap. 21). This conflation of the eyes of the poet's beloved with the eyes of the demon suggests, even more surely than the allusion to Eve, that the demon is the form, not only of Frankenstein's solipsism, of his need to obviate the mother, but also of the narcissism that constitutes the safety of the ego for whose sake the mother is denied. The monster is still the object of Frankenstein's desire when Elizabeth writes to him, just as its creation was the object of his initial quest. It is this monster, the monster of narcissism, that intervenes on the wedding night, substituting Frankenstein's desire for his own imagining for the consummation of his marriage, just as the visionary maiden in *Alastor* takes the place both of the dead Mother Nature of the poet's prologue and of the real maiden the hero meets, attracts, and rejects in the course of his quest.

That the demon is a revision of Eve, of emanations, and of the object of Romantic desire, is confirmed by its female attributes. Its very bodiliness, its identification with matter, associates it with traditional concepts of femaleness. Further, the impossibility of Frankenstein giving it a female demon, an object of its own desire, aligns the demon with women, who are forbidden to have their own desires. But if the demon is really a feminine object of desire, why is it a he? I would suggest that this constitutes part of Shelley's exposure of the male Romantic economy that would substitute for real and therefore powerful female others a being imagined on the model of the male poet's own self. By making the demon masculine, Shelley suggests that Romantic desire seeks to do away, not only with the mother, but also with all females so as to live finally in a world of mirrors that reflect a comforting illusion of the male self's independent wholeness. It is worth noting that just as Frankenstein's desire is for a male demon, Walton too yearns, not for a bride, but for "the company of a man who could sympathize with me, whose eyes would reply to mine" (letter 2).

It may seem peculiar to describe the demon as the object of Frankenstein's Romantic desire, since he spends most of the novel suffering from the demon's crimes. Yet in addition to the allusions to Eve and the "fleeting shade" in *Alastor* that suggest this, it is clear that while Frankenstein is in the process of creating the demon, he loves it and desires it; the knowledge that makes possible its creation is the "consummation" of his "toils." It is only when the demon becomes animated that Frankenstein abruptly discovers his loathing for his creation. Even though the demon looks at its creator with what appears to be love, Frankenstein's response to it is unequivocal loathing. Why had he never noticed before the hideousness of its shape and features? No adequate account is given, nor could be, for as we shall see, this is what most mystifies and horrifies Shelley about her own situation. Frankenstein confesses, "I had desired it with an ardour that far exceeded moderation; but now that I had finished, the beauty of the dream vanished, and breathless horror and disgust filled my heart" (chap. 5). The Romantic quest is always doomed, for it secretly resists its own fulfillment: although the hero of *Alastor* quests for his dream maiden and dies of not finding her, his encounter with the Indian maid makes it clear that embodiment is itself an obstacle to desire, or more precisely, its termination. Frankenstein's desire for his creation lasts only so long as that creation remains uncreated, the substitution for the too-powerful mother of a figure issuing from his imagination and therefore under his control.

. . . The predicament of Frankenstein, as of the hero of *Alastor*, is that of the son in Lacan's revision of the Freudian oedipal crisis. In flight from the body of the mother forbidden by the father, a maternal body that he sees as dead in his urgency to escape it and to enter a paternal order constituted of its distance from the mother, the son seeks figurations that will at once make restitution for the mother and confirm her death and absence by substituting for her figures that are under his control. Fundamentally, the son cannot wish for these figurative substitutes to be embodied, for any *body* is too reminiscent of the mother and is no longer under the son's control, as the demon's excessive strength demonstrates; the value of these figurations is that they remain figurations. In just this way, Romantic desire does not desire to be fulfilled, and yet, because it seems both to itself and to others to want to be embodied, the Romantic quester as son is often confronted with a body he seems to want but does not. Thus Frankenstein thinks he wants to create the demon, but when he has succeeded, he discovers that what he really enjoyed was the process leading up to the creation, the seemingly endless chain of signifiers that constitute his true, if unrecognized, desire.

Looking at *Alastor* through *Frankenstein*'s reading of it, then, we see that the novel is the story of a hypothetical case: what if the hero of *Alastor* actually got what he thinks he wants? What if desire were embodied, contrary to the poet's deepest wishes? That Shelley writes such a case suggests that this was her own predicament. In real life, Percy Shelley pursued her as the poet and hero of *Alastor* pursue ghosts and as Frankenstein pursues the secrets of the grave. That he courted the adolescent Mary Godwin at the grave of her mother, whose writing he admired, already suggests that the daughter was for him a figure for the safely dead mother, a younger and less powerfully creative version of her. Yet when he got this substitute, he began to tire of her, as he makes quite explicit in *Epipsychidion*, where he is not embarrassed to describe his life in terms of an interminable quest for an imaginary woman. Mary starts out in that poem as one "who seemed / As like the glorious shape which I had dreamed" (ll. 227–78) but soon becomes "that Moon" with "pale and waning lips" (l. 309). The poet does not seem to notice that each time an embodiment of the ideal turns out to be unsatisfactory, it is not because she is the wrong woman, but because the very fact of embodiment inevitably spoils the vision. Emily, the final term in the poem's sequence of women, remains ideal only because she has not yet been possessed, and indeed at the end of the poem, the poet disintegrates and disembodies her, perhaps to save himself from yet one more disappointment. Shelley was for herself never anything but embodied, but for Percy Shelley it seems to have been a grave disappointment to discover her substantiality, and therefore her inadequacy for fulfilling his visionary requirements. *Frankenstein* is the story of what it feels like to be the undesired embodiment of Romantic imaginative desire. The demon, rejected merely for being a body, suffers in something of the way that Shelley must have felt herself to suffer under the conflicting demands of Romantic desire: on the one hand, that she must embody the goal of Percy's quest, and on the other, his rejection of that embodiment.

Later in the novel, when the demon describes to Frankenstein its discovery and reading of the "journal of the four months that preceded my creation," the discrepancy between Percy's conflicting demands is brought to the fore. The demon notes that the journal records "the whole detail of that series of disgusting circumstances" that resulted in "my accursed origin," and that "the minutest description of my odious and loathsome person is given, in language which painted your own horrors and rendered mine indelible" (chap. 15). This summary suggests that while Frankenstein was writing the journal during the period leading up to the demon's vivification, he was fully aware of his creature's hideousness. Yet Frankenstein, in his own account of the same period, specifically says that it was only when "I had finished, the beauty of the dream vanished, and breathless horror and disgust filled my heart" (chap. 5). If Frankenstein is right about his feelings here, why should his journal be full of "language which painted [his] horrors"? Or, if the account in the journal is correct, if Frankenstein was aware from the start of his creature's "odious and loathsome person," why does he tell Walton that the demon appeared hideous to him only upon its awakening? If the text of this journal is, like *Alastor*, the record of a Romantic quest for an object of desire, then the novel is presenting us with two conflicting readings of the poem—Frankenstein's or Percy's and the demon's or Shelley's—confirming our sense that Shelley reading *Alastor* finds in it the story of Percy's failure to find in her the object of his desire, or the story of his desire not to find the object of his desire, not to find that she is the object.

A famous anecdote [related by John William Polidori in his diary] about the Shelleys from a few days after the beginning of the ghost story contest in which *Frankenstein* originated lends support to this impression of Shelley's experience. Byron was reciting some lines from Coleridge's *Christabel* about Geraldine, who is, like the demon, a composite body, half young and beautiful, half (in the version Byron recited) "hideous, deformed, and pale of hue." Percy, "suddenly shrieking and putting his hands to his head, ran out of the room with a candle." Brought to his senses, he told Byron and Polidori that "he was looking at Mrs. Shelley" while Byron was repeating Coleridge's lines, "and suddenly thought of a woman that he had heard of who had eyes instead of nipples." If disembodied eyes are, in *Alastor*, what are so alluring to the hero about his beloved, eyes in place of nipples may have been Percy's hallucination of the horror of having those ideal eyes reembodied in the form of his real lover. This is an embodiment that furthermore calls attention to its failure to be sufficiently different from the mother, whose nipples are for the baby so important a feature. An actual woman, who is herself a mother, does not fit the ideal of disembodied femininity, and the vision of combining real and ideal is a monster. Mary's sense of herself viewed as a collection of incongruent body parts—breasts terminating in eyes—might have found expression in the demon, whose undesirable corporeality is expressed as its being composed likewise of ill-fitting parts. *Paradise Lost, Alastor,* and other texts in this tradition compel women readers to wish to embody, as Eve does, imaginary ideals, to be glad of this role in masculine life; and yet at the same time, they warn women readers that they will suffer for such embodiment.

. . . The demon is about the ambivalent response of a woman reader to some of our culture's most compelling statements of woman's place in the myth. That the mother must vanish and be replaced by never quite embodied figures for her is equivalent to the vanishing of the referent (along with that time with the mother when the referent had not vanished) to be replaced by language as figuration that never quite touches its objects. Women's role is to be that silent or lost referent, the literal whose absence makes figuration possible. To be also the figurative substitute for that lost referent, is, Shelley shows, impossible, for women are constantly reminded that they are the mother's (loathed, loved) body, and in any case, "being" is incompatible with being a figure. The literal provokes horror in the male poet, or scientist, even while he demands that women literalize his vision.

That Shelley knew she was writing a criticism, not only of women's self-contradictory role in androcentric ontology, but also of the gendered myth of language that is part of that ontology, is suggested by the appearance of a series of images of writing at the very end of the novel. Once again, the demon is the object of Frankenstein's quest, pursued now in hate rather than in love. Frankenstein is preternaturally motivated in his quest by an energy of desire that recalls his passion when first creating the demon, and that his present quest depends on the killing of animals recalls his first quest's dependence on dead bodies. Frankenstein believes that "a spirit of good" follows and directs his steps: "Sometimes, when nature, overcome by hunger, sank under the exhaustion, a repast was prepared for me in the desert that restored and inspirited me. . . . I will not doubt that it was set there by the spirits that I had invoked to aid me" (chap. 24). He says this, however, directly after pointing out that the demon sometimes helped him. Fearing "that if I lost all trace of him I should despair and die, [he] left some mark to guide me," and Frankenstein also notes that the demon would frequently leave "marks in writing on the barks of the trees or cut in stone that guided me and instigated my fury." One of these messages includes the information, "You will find near this place, if you follow not too tardily, a dead hare; eat and be refreshed." Frankenstein, it would seem, deliberately misinterprets the demon's guidance and provisions for him as belonging instead to a spirit of good: his interpretation of the demon's marks and words is so figurative as to be opposite to what they really say. The demon, all body, writes appropriately on the body of nature messages that refer, if to objects at a distance, at least at not a very great distance ("you will find near this place"). Frankenstein, however, reads as figuratively as possible, putting as great a distance as possible between what he actually reads and what he interprets. His reading furthermore puts a distance between himself and the object of his quest, which he still cannot desire to attain; figurative reading would extend indefinitely the pleasure of the quest itself by forever putting off the moment of capture. Just at the moment when Frankenstein thinks he is about to reach the demon, the demon is transformed from a "mark," as if a mark on a page, into a "form," and Frankenstein seeks to reverse this transformation. One of Frankenstein's sled dogs has died of exhaustion, delaying him; "suddenly my eye caught a dark speck upon the dusky plain"; he utters "a wild cry of ecstasy" upon "distinguish[ing] a sledge and the distorted proportions of a well-known form within" (chap. 24).

Frankenstein's response, however, is to take an hour's rest: his real aim, which he does not admit, is to keep the demon at the distance where he remains a "dark speck," a mark on the white page of the snow, his signification forever deferred.

At the same time that *Frankenstein* is about a woman writer's response to the ambiguous imperative her culture imposes upon her, it is also possible that the novel concerns a woman writer's anxieties about bearing children, about generating bodies that . . . would have the power to displace or kill the parent. Ellen Moers first opened up a feminist line of inquiry into the novel by suggesting that it is a "birth myth," that the horror of the demon is Shelley's horror, not only at her own depressing experience of childbirth, but also at her knowledge of the disastrous consequences of giving birth (or of pregnancy itself) for many women in her vicinity. The list is by now familiar to Shelley's readers. First, Mary Wollstonecraft died eleven days after she gave birth to Mary; then, during the time of the writing of the novel, Fanny Imlay, Mary's half-sister, drowned herself in October 1816 when she learned that she was her mother's illegitimate child by Gilbert Imlay; Harriet Shelley was pregnant by another man when she drowned herself in the Serpentine in December 1816; and Claire Clairmont, the daughter of the second Mrs. Godwin, was, scandalously, pregnant by Byron, much to the embarrassment of the Shelleys, with whom she lived. Illegitimate pregnancy, that is, a pregnancy over which the woman has particularly little control, brings either death to the mother in childbirth (Wollstonecraft) or shame, making visible what ought to have remained out of sight, the scene of conception (Claire), a shame that can itself result in the death of both mother (Harriet Shelley) and child (Fanny).

At the time of the conception of the novel, Mary Godwin had herself borne two illegitimate children: the first, an unnamed girl, died four days later, in March 1815; the second was five months old. In December 1816, when Harriet Shelley died and Shelley had finished chapter 4 of the novel, she was pregnant again. With but a single parent, the demon in her novel is the world's most monstrously illegitimate child, and this illegitimate child causes the death of that parent as well as of the principle of motherhood, as we have seen. Read in connection with the history of disastrous illegitimacies, the novel's logic would seem to be this: to give birth to an illegitimate child is monstrous, for it is the inexorable life of these babies, especially those of Mary Wollstonecraft and of Harriet Shelley, that destroys the life of the mother. Subsequently, as Marc Rubenstein argues, the guilty daughter pays for the destruction of her own mother in a fantasy of being destroyed by her own child.

In *Jane Eyre* and *Wuthering Heights*, . . . the image of childbirth is associated with the uncontrollability of real things. Once a conception has taken objective form, it has the power to destroy its own source, to transform the mother herself into the literal. In the Brontës' novels, childbirth is structurally equivalent to (and indeed also often situated in) the coming true of dreams, which has, like childbirth, an ironic relation to the original conception. Shelley's 1831 introduction to her novel makes a comparable equation of giving birth, the realization of a dream, and writing. As many readers have pointed out, this introduction to her revised version of the novel identifies the novel itself with the demon, and both with a child. She tells of being asked every morning if she had thought of a story, as if a story, like a baby, were necessarily to be conceived in the privacy of the night. And at the close of the introduction she writes, "I bid my hideous progeny go forth and prosper," and she refers to the novel in the next sentence as "the offspring of happy days." The genesis of the novel, furthermore, is in a dream that she transcribes, a dream moreover that is about the coming true of a dream. One night, she says, after listening to conversation about the reanimation of corpses, "Night waned upon this talk. . . . When I placed my head on my pillow I did not sleep, nor could I be said to think. My imagination, unbidden, possessed and guided me." Then follows her account of the famous dream of "the pale student of unhallowed arts kneeling beside the thing he had put together," the "hideous phantasm of a man" stirring "with an uneasy, half-vital motion," and the "artist" sleeping and waking to behold "the horrid thing . . . looking on him with yellow, watery, but speculative eyes." Waking in horror from her dream, she at first tries "to think of something else," but then realizes that she has the answer to her need for a ghost story: " 'What terrified me will terrify others; and I need only describe the spectre which had haunted my midnight pillow.' . . . I began that day with the words, 'It was on a dreary night of November,' making only a transcript of the grim terrors of my waking dream." Making a transcript of a dream—that is, turning an idea into the "machinery of a story"—a dream that is about the transformation of a "phantasm" into a real body, is equivalent here to conceiving a child. She makes it very clear that her dream takes the place of a sexual act ("Night waned. . . . When I placed my head on my pillow . . . I saw the pale student"), just as the book idea she can announce the next day substitutes for a baby. The terrifying power of the possibility that her dream might be true encodes the terrifying power of conception and childbirth. In Deutsch's language, "she who has created this new life must obey its power; its rule is expected, yet invisible, implacable." [*Motherhood*].

Despite Ellen Moers's delineation of the resemblance of the demon to the apprehensions a mother might have about a baby, it is the introduction that supplies the most explicit evidence for identifying demon and book with a child. Mary Poovey has demonstrated that this introduction has a significantly different ideological cast from the original version of the novel (or even from the revised novel). Written in 1831, fourteen years after the novel itself and following the death of Percy Shelley (as well as the deaths of both the children who were alive or expected in 1816–17), the introduction takes pains to distance itself from the novel, and it aims to bring the writing of the novel further within the fold of the conventional domestic life Shelley retrospectively substitutes for the radically disruptive life she in fact led. Referring obliquely to her elopement with Percy and its effect on her adolescent habit of inventing stories, for example, she writes, "After this my life became busier, and reality stood in place of fiction." Echoed later by Robert Southey's remark to Charlotte Brontë, that "literature cannot be the business of a woman's life," Shelley's busyness refers largely to her responsibilities as a mother and wife. When she describes her endeavor to write a ghost story she repeats this term for family responsibility: "I busied myself *to think of a story*." This echo suggests that her busyness with story writing is somehow congruent with, not in conflict with, her "busier" life as a wife and mother. It makes the novel, "so very hideous an idea," seem somehow part of the busy life of a matron. It is this effort, to domesticate her hideous idea, that may be at the bottom of her characterizing it as a "hideous progeny." If the novel read in this light seems, like *Jane Eyre* and *Wuthering Heights*, to be full of a horror of childbirth, that may only be the result of the impossibility of changing the basic story of the 1817 novel, the result of assembling mismatched parts.

Thus the novel may be about the horror associated with motherhood, yet this reading seems unduly influenced by the superimpositions of the introduction, and furthermore it ignores the novel's most prominent feature, that the demon is not a child born of woman but the creation of a man. Most succinctly put, the novel is about the collision between androcentric and gynocentric theories of creation, a collision that results in the denigration of maternal childbearing through its circumvention by male creation. The novel presents Mary Shelley's response to the expectation, manifested in such poems as *Alastor* or *Paradise Lost*, that women embody and yet not embody male fantasies. At the same time, it expresses a woman's knowledge of the irrefutable independence of the body, both her own and those of the children that she produces, from projective male fantasy. While a masculine being— God, Adam, Percy Shelley, Frankenstein—may imagine that his creation of an imaginary being may remain under the control of his desires, Mary Shelley knows otherwise, both through her experience as mistress and wife of Percy and through her experience of childbirth. Shelley's particular history shows irrefutably that children, even pregnancies, do not remain under the control of those who conceive them.

Keats writes that "the Imagination may be compared to Adam's dream—he awoke and found it truth." In *Paradise Lost*, narrating his recollection of Eve's creation, Adam describes how he fell into a special sleep—"Mine eyes he clos'd, but op'n left the Cell / Of Fancy my internal sight" (8.460–61)—then watched, "though sleeping," as God formed a creature,

> Manlike, but different sex, so lovely fair,
> That what seem'd fair in all the World, seem'd now
> Mean, or in her summ'd up.
>
> (8.471–73)

This is "Adam's dream." But what of "he awoke and found it truth"? Adam wakes, "To find her, or for ever to deplore / Her loss" (ll. 479–80), and then, "behold[s] her, not far off, / Such as I saw her in my dream" (ll. 481–82), yet what Keats represses is that the matching of reality to dream is not so neat as these lines suggest. Eve comes to Adam, not of her own accord, but "Led by her Heav'nly Maker" (l. 485), and as soon as he catches sight of her, Adam sees Eve turn away from him, an action he ascribes to modesty (and thus endeavors to assimilate to his dream of her) but that Eve, in book 4, has already said stemmed from her preference for her image in the water. Though designed by God for Adam "exactly to thy heart's desire" (8.451), Eve once created has a mind and will of her own, and this independence is so horrifying to the male imagination that the Fall is ascribed to it.

It is neither the visionary male imagination alone that Mary Shelley protests, then, nor childbirth itself, but the circumvention of the maternal creation of new beings by the narcissistic creations of male desire. While Keats can gloss over the discrepancy between Adam's dream and its fulfillment, Shelley cannot. As Frankenstein is on the verge of completing the female demon, it is for her resemblance to Eve that he destroys her. Just as Adam says of Eve, "seeing me, she turn'd" (8.507), Frankenstein fears the female demon's turning from the demon toward a more attractive image: "She also might turn with disgust from him to the superior beauty of man" (chap. 20). Also like Eve, who disobeys a prohibition agreed upon between Adam and God before her creation, she "might refuse to comply with a compact made before her creation," the demon's promise to leave Europe. Frankenstein typifies the way in which the biological creation of necessarily imperfect yet independent beings has always been made to seem, within an androcentric economy, monstrous and alarming. Although Mary Wollstonecraft would in any case have died of puerperal fever after Mary's birth, her earlier pregnancy with Fanny and the pregnancies of Harriet Shelley, Claire Clairmont, and Mary Godwin would have done no harm had they not been labeled "illegitimate" by a society that places a premium on the ownership by a man of his wife's body and children. The novel criticizes, not childbirth itself, but the male horror of independent embodiment. This permits us to speculate that the horror of childbirth in *Jane Eyre* and *Wuthering Heights* stems from the Brontës' identification with an androcentric perspective. To a certain extent, as a writer in a culture that defines writing as a male activity and as opposite to motherhood, Shelley too must share the masculine perspective, with its horror of embodiment and its perennial reenacting of Adam's affront at Eve's turning away. For whatever reason, however, perhaps because of her direct experience of the mother's position, Shelley is able to discern the androcentrism in her culture's view of the relation of childbearing to writing, and thus she enables us to interpret her own painful exposure of it.

At the site of the collision between motherhood and Romantic projection another form of literalization appears as well. While it is important how Shelley reads texts such as *Alastor* and *Paradise Lost*, it is also important to consider, perhaps more simply, that her novel reads them. Like the Brontës' novels, whose Gothic embodiments of subjective states, realizations of dreams, and literalized figures all literalize Romantic projection, Shelley's novel literalizes Romantic imagination, but with a different effect and to a different end. Shelley criticizes these texts by enacting them, and because enactment or embodiment is both the desire and the fear of such texts, the mode of her criticism matters. Just as the heroes of these poems seem to seek, but do not seek, embodiments of their visionary desires, these poetic texts seem to seek embodiment in "the machinery of a story." For in the ideology of post-romantic culture, it is part of a woman's duty to transcribe and give form to men's words, just as it is her duty to give form to their desire, or birth to their seed, no matter how ambivalently men may view the results of such projects. In the same passage in the introduction to the novel in which Shelley makes the analogy between the book and a child, between the conception of a story and the conception of a baby, and between these things and the coming true of a dream, she also identifies all these projects with the transcription of important men's words. Drawing on the ideology of maternity as the process of passing on a male idea, Shelley describes her book-child as the literalization of two poets' words:

> Many and long were the conversations between Lord Byron and Shelley to which I was a devout but nearly silent listener. During one of these, various philosophical doctrines were discussed, and among others the nature of the principle of life, and whether there was any probability of its ever being discovered and communicated. . . . Perhaps a corpse would be reanimated; galvanism had given token of such things: perhaps the component parts of a creature might be manufactured, brought together, and endued with vital warmth.

Directly following this passage appears her account of going to bed and vividly dreaming of the "student of unhallowed arts" and the "hideous phantasm," the dream of which she says she made "only a transcript" in transferring it into the central scene of her novel, the dream that equates the conception of a book with the conception of a child.

Commentators on the novel have in the past taken Shelley at her word here, believing, if not in her story of transcribing a dream, then certainly in her fiction of transcribing men's words. Mario Praz, for example, writes, "All Mrs. Shelley did was to provide a passive reflection of some of the wild fantasies which, as it were, hung in the air about her" [*The Romantic Agony*]. Harold Bloom suggests that "what makes *Frankenstein* an important book" despite its "clumsiness" is "that it contains one of the most vivid versions we have of the Romantic mythology of the self, one that resembles Blake's *Book of Urizen*, Shelley's *Prometheus Unbound*, and Byron's *Manfred*, among other works." It is part of the subtlety of her strategy to disguise her criticism of such works as a passive transcription, to appear to be a docile wife and "devout listener" to the conversations of important men. Indeed, central to her critical method is the practice of acting out docilely what these men tell her they want from her, to show them the consequences of their desires. She removes herself beyond reproach for "putting [her]self forward," by formulating her critique as a devout transcription, a "passive reflection," a "version" that "resembles." She inserts this authorial role into her novel in the form of a fictive M. S., Walton's sister, Margaret Saville, to whom his letters containing Frankenstein's story are sent and who silently records and transmits them to the reader.

Now that we have assembled the parts of Shelley's introductory account of the novel's genesis, we can see she equates childbearing with the bearing of men's words. Writing a transcript of a dream that was in turn merely the transcript of a conversation is also giving birth to a hideous progeny conceived in the night. The conversation between Byron and Shelley probably represents Shelley's and Byron's poetry, the words, for example, for *Alastor* that she literalizes in her novel. That the notion of motherhood as the passive transcription of men's words is at work here is underscored by the allusion this idea makes to the Christ story. "Perhaps a corpse would be reanimated" refers initially, not to science's power, but to that occasion, a myth but surely still a powerful one even in this den of atheists, when a corpse was reanimated, which is in turn an allusion to the virgin birth. Like the creations of Adam and Eve, which excluded the maternal, Christ's birth bypassed the normal channels of procreation. It is this figure, whose birth is also the literalization of a masculine God's Word, who serves as the distant prototype for the reanimation of corpses. And within the fiction, the demon too is the literalization of a word, an idea, Frankenstein's theory given physical form. As Joyce Carol Oates remarks, the demon "is a monster-son born of Man exclusively, a parody of the Word or Idea made Flesh." The book-baby literalizes Shelley's and Byron's words, the words of their conversation as figures for Shelley's words in *Alastor*, just as the demon-baby literalizes Frankenstein's inseminating words. Christ literalizes God's Word through the medium of a woman, Mary, who passively transmits Word into flesh without being touched by it. Literalizations again take place through the medium of a more recent Mary, who passively transcribes (or who seems to), who adds nothing but "the platitude of prose" and "the machinery of a story" to the words of her more illustrious male companions who for their own writing prefer "the music of the most melodious verse." And yet, . . . it is precisely the adding of this "machinery," which would seem only to facilitate the transmission of the ideas and figures of poetry into the more approachable form of a story, that subverts and reverses what it appears so passively to serve.

The demon literalizes the male Romantic poet's desire for a figurative object of desire, but it also literalizes the literalization of male literature. While telling Frankenstein the story of its wanderings and of its education by the unknowing cottagers, the demon reports having discovered in the woods "a leathern portmanteau containing. . . . some books. I eagerly seized the prize and returned with it to my hovel" (chap. 15). The discovery of these books—*Paradise Lost*, Plutarch's *Lives*, and *The Sorrows of Werther*—is followed in the narrative, but preceded in represented time, by the demon's discovery of another book, Frankenstein's "journal of the four months that preceded [the demon's] creation." Both *Frankenstein*, the book as baby, and the demon as baby literalize these books, especially *Paradise Lost*—the demon is Satan, Adam, and Eve, while Frankenstein himself is Adam, Satan, and God—as well as a number of other prior texts, among them, as we have seen, *Alastor*, but also the book of Genesis, Coleridge's "Rime of the Ancient Mariner," Aeschylus's *Prometheus Bound*, Wordsworth's "Tintern Abbey," William Godwin's *Caleb Williams*, and many others. At the same time and in the same way, the demon is the realization of Frankenstein's words in the journal of his work on the demon, a journal that is in some ways equivalent to (or a literalization of) *Alastor*, since both record a Romantic quest for what was "desired . . . with an ardor that far exceeded moderation." The demon, wandering about the woods of Germany carrying these books, the book of his own physical origin and the texts that contribute to his literary origin, embodies the very notion of literalization with which everything about him seems to be identified. To carry a book is exactly what Mary Shelley does in bearing the words of the male authors, in giving birth to a hideous progeny that is at once book and demon. Carrying the books of his own origin, the demon emblematizes the literalization of literature that Shelley, through him, practices.

I pointed out earlier that Mary Shelley, unlike the Brontës, would not see childbirth itself as inherently threatening apart from the interference in it by a masculine economy. Likewise, writing or inventing stories is not inherently monstrous—witness her retrospective account in the introduction of how, before her life became "busier," she used to "commune with the creatures of my fancy" and compose unwritten stories out of doors: "It was beneath the trees of the grounds belonging to our house, or on the bleak sides of the woodless mountain near, that my true compositions, the airy flights of my imagination, were born and fostered." Like both Cathys in *Wuthering Heights* in their childhood, indeed, probably like the young Brontës themselves, Mary Shelley's imagination prior to the fall into the Law of the Father—in her case, elopement, pregnancy, and marriage—is at one with nature and also does not require to be written down. The metaphor of composition as childbirth—"my true compositions . . . were born and fostered"—appears here as something not only harmless but celebratory. It is only when both childbirth and a woman's invention of stories are subordinated to the Law of the Father that they become monstrous; it is only when such overpowering and masculinist texts as Genesis, *Paradise Lost*, and *Alastor* appropriate this Mary's body, her female power of embodiment, as vehicle for the transmission of their words, that monsters are born. When God appropriates maternal procreation in Genesis or *Paradise Lost*, a beautiful object is created; but through the reflex of Mary Shelley's critique male circumvention of the maternal creates a monster. Her monster constitutes a criticism of such appropriation and circumvention, yet it is a criticism written in her own blood, carved in the very body of her own victimization, just as the demon carves words about death in the trees and rocks of the Arctic. She is powerless to stop her own appropriation and can only demonstrate the pain that appropriation causes in the woman reader and writer.

Chronology

1797   Mary Wollstonecraft Godwin Shelley born August 30 at Somers Town, daughter of the radical philosopher William Godwin and the even more radical writer and feminist Mary Wollstonecraft, who dies ten days later.

1801   William Godwin is remarried to a widow, Mary Jane Clairmont, mother of two children, Charles and Jane, later known as Claire Clairmont.

1812   First meeting with Shelley, November 11.

1814   Meets Shelley again in London. Elopes with him to France and Switzerland, accompanied by Claire Clairmont. Returns with him to England.

1815   In February, Mary gives birth to a premature girl child, who dies two weeks later.

1816   Birth of son William in January. In May, the Shelleys and Claire depart from England to Geneva, where Byron awaits Claire. In July, they visit Mont Blanc. *Frankenstein* begun. September sees return to England. In October, Fanny Imlay, daughter of Mary Wollstonecraft, kills herself. This is followed in December by the suicide of Harriet Shelley, the poet's first wife. Mary is married to Shelley in London on December 30.

1817   The Shelleys move to Marlow. *Frankenstein* finished in May. Birth of daughter, Clara. *History of a Six-Weeks' Tour* published.

1818   Departure of Shelley household to Italy in March. Publication of *Frankenstein*. Clara dies in Venice, in September, during a visit of the Shelleys to Byron. They go south, first to Rome, and then to Naples for the winter.

155

1819   Writes *Mathilda*. Death of her son William in Rome, in March. In November, her son Percy Florence is born. He is to be the Shelleys' only survivor.

1820   Residence in Leghorn and Pisa.

1821   The Shelleys join with Edward and Jane Williams, at Pisa, with Byron close by. Love affair of Shelley and Jane Williams.

1822   Move to Casa Magni, near Lerici. Death of Percy Bysshe Shelley and Edward Williams in July, when the poet's sail-boat, *The Ariel*, is lost at sea. In September, the widowed Mary joins Byron and Leigh Hunt at Genoa.

1823   *Valperga* published. Return to London in August.

1824   Publication of Mary's edition of Shelley's *Posthumous Poems*. The volume withdrawn when Sir Timothy Shelley, the poet's father, raises objections.

1826   *The Last Man* published.

1830   *Perkin Warbeck* published.

1835   *Lodore* published.

1836   Death of her father, William Godwin.

1837   *Falkner* published.

1844   *Rambles in Germany and Italy* published.

1851   Dies February 1 in London.

1959   *Mathilda* first published.

Contributors

HAROLD BLOOM, Sterling Professor of the Humanities at Yale University, is the author of *The Anxiety of Influence, Poetry and Repression*, and many other volumes of literary criticism. His forthcoming study, *Freud: Transference and Authority*, attempts a full-scale reading of all of Freud's major writings. A MacArthur Prize Fellow, he is general editor of five series of literary criticism published by Chelsea House.

GEORGE LEVINE, Professor of English at Rutgers University, is the author of *The Boundaries of Fiction, The Realistic Imagination*, and is coeditor, with U. C. Knoepflmacher, of *The Endurance of Frankenstein*.

PAUL SHERWIN is Dean of Humanities and Professor of English at the City College of the City University of New York. He is the author of *Precious Bane: Collins and the Miltonic Legacy*.

BARBARA JOHNSON is Professor of Romance Languages and Literature at Harvard University. She is the author of *Défigurations du langage poétique* and *The Critical Difference*, and co-author of a forthcoming study on Zora Neale Hurston. She is also editor of *The Pedagogical Imperative: Teaching as a Literary Genre* and the translator of Jacques Derrida's *Dissemination*.

JOYCE CAROL OATES, prolific novelist, poet, and critic, is Professor of English at Princeton University. Her most recent work includes the novel *Marya* and *The Profane Art*, a collection of essays.

MARY POOVEY, Professor of English at Rutgers University, is the author of *The Proper Lady and the Woman Writer: Ideology as Style in the Works of Mary Wollstonecraft, Mary Shelley and Jane Austen*.

WILLIAM VEEDER is Professor of English at the University of Chicago. He is the author of books on Yeats, Henry James, and Victorian

157

feminism, as well as of *Mary Shelley and Frankenstein: The Fate of Androgyny*.

MARGARET HOMANS is Associate Professor of English at Yale University. She is the author of *Women Writers and Poetic Identity: Dorothy Wordsworth, Emily Bronte and Emily Dickinson* and of *Bearing the Word: Language and Female Experience in Nineteenth-Century Women's Writing*.

Bibliography

Bloom, Harold, ed. *Modern Critical Views: Mary Shelley*. New York: Chelsea House, 1985.

Brooks, Peter. " 'Godlike Science/Unhallowed Arts': Language and Monstrosity in *Frankenstein*." *New Literary History* 9 (1977): 591–605.

Church, Richard. *Mary Shelley*. London: Gerald Howe, 1928.

Cude, Wilfred. "Mary Shelley's Modern Prometheus: A Study in the Ethics of Scientific Creativity." *Dalhousie Review* 52 (1972): 212–25.

Dunn, Jane. *Moon in Eclipse: A Life of Mary Shelley*. New York: St. Martin's, 1978.

Dussinger, John A. "Kinship and Guilt in Mary Shelley's *Frankenstein*." *Studies in the Novel* 8 (1976): 38–55.

Fleck, P. D. "Mary Shelley's Notes to Shelley's Poems and *Frankenstein*." *Studies in Romanticism* 6 (1967): 226–54.

Gilbert, Sandra. "Horror's Twin: Mary Shelley's Monstrous Eve." *Feminist Studies* 4 (1978): 48–73. Reprinted in Sandra M. Gilbert and Susan Gubar, *The Madwoman in the Attic: The Woman Writer and the Nineteenth-Century Imagination*. New Haven: Yale University Press, 1979.

Glut, Donald F. *The Frankenstein Legend: A Tribute to Mary Shelley and Boris Karloff*. Metuchen, N.J.: Scarecrow, 1973.

Grylls, Rosalie. *Mary Shelley: A Biography*. London: Oxford University Press, 1938.

Harris Smith, Susan. "*Frankenstein*: Mary Shelley's Psychic Divisiveness." *Women and Literature* 5 (1977): 42–53.

Hill, J. M. "*Frankenstein* and the Physiognomy of Desire." *American Imago* 32 (1975): 332–58

Hirsch, Gordon D. "The Monster Was a Lady: On the Psychology of Mary Shelley's *Frankenstein*." *Hartford Studies in Literature* 7 (1975): 116–53.

Hodges, Devon. "*Frankenstein* and the Feminine Subversion of the Novel." *Tulsa Studies in Women's Literature* 2 (Fall 1983): 155–64.

Jacobus, Mary. "Is There a Woman in This Text?" *New Literary History* 13 (1982): 117–41.

Jones, Frederick L., ed. *The Letters of Mary W. Shelley*. 2 vols. Norman: University of Oklahoma Press, 1946.

———. *Mary Shelley's Journal*. Norman: University of Oklahoma Press, 1947.

Kaplan, Morton, and Robert Kloss. "Fantasy of Paternity and the Doppelgänger: Mary Shelley's *Frankenstein.*" In *The Unspoken Motive: A Guide to Psychoanalytic Literary Criticism.* New York: Free Press, 1973.

Ketterer, Alphonse. *Frankenstein's Creation: The Book, the Monster, and Human Reality.* ELS Monograph Series 16, Victoria, B.C.: University of Victoria, 1979.

Kieley, Robert. *The Romantic Novel in England.* Cambridge: Harvard University Press, 1972.

Levine, George. "*Frankenstein* and the Tradition of Realism." *Novel* 7 (1973): 14–30.

Levine, George, and U. C. Knoepflmacher, eds. *The Endurance of Frankenstein.* Berkeley: University of California Press, 1979.

McInerney, Peter. "*Frankenstein* and the Godlike Science of Letters." *Genre* 13 (1980) 455–75.

Marshall, Mrs. Julian. *The Life and Letters of Mary Wollstonecraft Shelley.* 2 vols. London: Richard Bentley, 1889.

Miyoshi, Masao. *The Divided Self: A Perspective on the Literature of the Victorians.* New York: New York University Press, 1969.

Moers, Ellen. *Literary Women.* New York: Doubleday, 1977.

Nelson, Lowry, Jr. "Night Thoughts on the Gothic Novel." *Yale Review* 52 (1962) 236–57.

Nitchie, Elizabeth. *Mary Shelley: Author of* Frankenstein. New Brunswick, N.J.: Rutgers University Press, 1953.

Norman, Sylvia. "Mary Wollstonecraft Shelley." In *Shelley and His Circle,* edited by Kenneth Neill Cameron, vol. 3. Cambridge: Harvard University Press, 1961, 1970.

Pollin, Burton R. "Philosophical and Literary Sources of *Frankenstein.*" *Comparative Literature* 17 (1965): 87–108.

Poovey, Mary. "My Hideous Progeny: Mary Shelley and the Feminization of Romanticism." *PMLA* 95 (1980): 332–47.

Rieger, James, ed. *Frankenstein, or The Modern Prometheus (The 1818 Text).* Chicago: University of Chicago Press, 1982.

Rubenstein, Marc A. " 'My Accursed Origin': The Search for the Mother in *Frankenstein.*" *Studies in Romanticism* 15 (1976): 165–94.

Seed, David. "*Frankenstein:* Parable or Spectacle?" *Criticism* 24 (1982): 327–40.

Small, Christopher. *Mary Shelley's Frankenstein.* Pittsburgh: University of Pittsburgh Press, 1973. Originally published as *Ariel like a Harpy: Shelley, Mary and Frankenstein.*

Spark, Muriel. *Child of Light: A Reassessment of Mary Wollstonecraft Shelley.* Essex, England: Tower Bridge Publications, 1951.

Spivak, Gayatri Chakravorty. "Three Women's Texts and a Critique of Imperialism." *Critical Inquiry* 12 (1985): 243–61.

Tillotson, Marcia. "A Forced Solitude: Mary Shelley and the Creation of Frankenstein's Monster." In *The Female Gothic,* edited by Julian E. Fleenor. Montreal: Eden, 1983.

Todd, Janet M., ed. *Wollstonecraft Anthology.* Bloomington: Indiana University Press, 1977.

Wade, Philip. "Shelley and the Miltonic Element in Mary Shelley's *Frankenstein*." *Milton and the Romantics* 2 (1976): 23–25.

Walling, William A. *Mary Shelley*. New York: Twayne, 1972.

Wilt, Judith. *Ghosts of the Gothic: Austen, Eliot, and Lawrence*. Princeton: Princeton University Press, 1980.

Acknowledgments

"The Pattern: *Frankenstein* and Austen to Conrad" by George Levine from *The Realistic Imagination: English Fiction from* Frankenstein *to* Lady Chatterley by George Levine, © 1981 by the University of Chicago. Reprinted by permission of the author and the University of Chicago Press.

"*Frankenstein*: Creation as Catastrophe" by Paul Sherwin from *PMLA* 96, no. 5 (October 1981), © 1981 by the Modern Language Association of America. Reprinted by permission of the Modern Language Association of America.

"My Monster/My Self" by Barbara Johnson from *Diacritics* 12, no. 2 (Summer 1982), © 1982 by the Johns Hopkins University Press, Baltimore/ London. Reprinted by permission.

"Frankenstein's Fallen Angel" by Joyce Carol Oates from *Critical Inquiry* 10, no. 3 (March 1984), © 1984 by the University of Chicago. Reprinted by permission of the author and the University of Chicago Press.

" 'My Hideous Progeny': The Lady and the Monster" by Mary Poovey from *The Proper Lady and the Woman Writer* by Mary Poovey, © 1984 by the University of Chicago. Reprinted by permission of the author and the University of Chicago Press.

"The Negative Oedipus: Father, *Frankenstein*, and the Shelleys" by William Veeder from *Critical Inquiry* 12, no. 2 (Winter 1986), © 1986 by the University of Chicago. Reprinted by permission of the author and the University of Chicago Press.

"Bearing Demons: Frankenstein's Circumvention of the Maternal" by Margaret Homans from *Bearing the Word: Language and Female Experience in Nineteenth-Century Women's Writing* by Margaret Homans, © 1986 by the University of Chicago. Reprinted by permission of the author and the University of Chicago Press.

Index